Two Cops and a Robber

Jill Owens

First Edition 2020

ISBN-13: 978-1-9163212-5-0

Fortis Publishing
Kemp House
160 City Road
London
EC1V 2NX

This book is a true story. Names have been not been changed and all events have been portrayed as accurately as my human memory was able to recall.

For Frankie

Acknowledgements

To Rod…My scaffold, my love, my hero.

To my children…My arms are always open.

To Peter…Lay those ghosts to rest my friend. They may have won the battle but they never won the war.

To Jennifer Jane…My sister in arms. Jump around.

To Annie Ann...For helping get my ducks in a row.

To Ken Scott. My mentor. Space. Full stop.

www.kenscottbooks.com

Matar a Goliat – Slay Goliath

Preface

This is a lot more than simply my first book. It's a
book of life. My life. It is also a book of hope.

Hope that one day more people will realise that
talking about personal, real-life issues is not
something to be ashamed of or kept secret, it is the
only way that recovery can commence.

We are none of us perfect, we are human. But being
human does not give people the excuse or the right
to destroy the happiness or the lives of others. Big
organisations may talk the talk of valuing and
supporting its employees, but sadly some don't walk

the walk. When you drill down deeper into the murky waters there is still evidence of the 'old boys Police club', officially outdated but in reality, very much alive and kicking.

Rules should apply to all. Rank or gender alone should not bring immunity, favour, penalty or escape routes.

Dyfed Powys Police, I was always coming back for you with my truth.

This is not a book about bitterness or revenge. I have not suddenly become the heroine while everyone else is the enemy. I don't want sympathy. Sympathy doesn't solve problems.

My story covers details from my perspective, which no doubt some may feel are too explicit or close to home and should remain hidden. But from discomfort comes progress. Progress nurtures strength. And strength brings that hope and the realisation that the comeback-kid within you is never too far away.

1

Halloween

One night. An ordinary weekday night that left a rancid, festering scar of pandemic proportion. Hacked into the walls of my memory, it sometimes fades. Mercifully. But when the trigger is squeezed, it opens and spews a million emotions.

The solid thump on the front door accompanied by screaming was not unexpected.

As I approached, I could just make out through the frosted glass the dark, menacing figures swarming around the front doorstep like moths around a flame. Googly eyes squinting through the glass and nostrils pressed so close they looked like smoking tunnels trying to melt their way through to peek inside.

Two sets of spaghetti legs came hurtling down the stairs. My girls, just twelve and seven, leaping the last two flights like flying bats and landing on top of each other in a screaming heap on the floor. I watched as they drew a large anticipatory intake of breath, the rush of air so pronounced it raised their eyelids like tiny drawbridges. Their hearts were beating out of their chests, eyes wide, peeking through the fan of fingers covering their faces. I slowly unlocked the door and it juddered open, sticking on its warped frame.

What I saw there was not pleasant.

Blood. Bloodied silhouettes, the faces obscured with masks.

Then screams.

'Just give it to them Mummy,' my girls shrieked, eyes wide open like saucers. As I heard the familiar, muffled words ooze from behind the masks I knew it was time.

Time to hand over what they wanted into their outstretched and grabbing hands.

'Trick or treat, Mrs…time to hand over the goodies!'

It was Halloween, 31 October 2006. An ordinary, crisp but spectacularly ghoulish night.

On the pavement outside my conventional three-bedroom semi-detached house on an average housing estate, the streetlamps held court and gave everything a weird, tangerine glow.

The frost was slowly creeping, the air outside resembling the guts of a giant freezer with the chilled haze descending on the shivering, manicured lawns. The blades of grass rigid, like tiny daggers wrapped in a white, sugary coat.

Inside the windows the fired, mutilated pumpkins matched the menacing mood perfectly. At the neighbour's place opposite, the creepy life-size waiter stood to attention at the front door as he did every year. Black dusty dinner suit, lit lantern hoisted in the air illuminating his haggard grey face, cobweb like hair and toothless grin. His features so lifelike, you had to do a double take and squint to make sure he wasn't actually moving.

As a child I had never really enjoyed or participated in Halloween, not through choice but simply because, 'it was stupid, commercialised American crap, in fact it is begging, and you are not to be seen doing that.'

The words of my father who always made a habit of knowing best how to encourage an immeasurable amount of fun. So, the door was never answered and instead, the mission was to make sure all the lights were off. If there was a knock, often on the kitchen window too for good measure, we had to keep as quiet as mice. No movement, yet strategically positioned to peek out from behind the thick, drawn curtains to make sure that Frankenstein and the monster crew were not trashing the family car. It was more like a stake-out. No pumpkins and definitely no sweets to sneak from the goody bucket as a compromise.

With my two girls I wanted things to be different and although they loved the thought of Halloween, it nevertheless scared the living daylights out of them every time they heard the rickety latch click upwards on the front gate.

The hot dogs or *witches' fingers* and blood red ketchup were going down a treat when my mobile rang.

It was Dean.

'Hey gorgeous, just checking in on you all. How's my beautiful boy?'

We were expecting our son. I too was pumpkin-like at 16 weeks pregnant. Life, it seemed, could not get much better.

We had met through an online dating site. At that time this way of finding love still carried a 'stigma' and was supposedly used only by 'desperate people'. Often that perception was generated by those who had no experience of the sites and were not looking for a partner to enrich their lives with happiness.

I did not view it like that. I thought it was a safer, more selective means of dating without having to commit to the drama and possible danger of an actual date with a complete stranger.

Udate was quite entertaining and it helped pass the

winter evenings when the kids were in bed. However it wasn't completely fool proof against those of a more eccentric perspective or in my terminology, 'weirdos'.

I quickly became an expert as to how it all worked and learned that I had to be myself and cut to the chase to avoid a lot of wasted effort. I had viewed so many profiles, pictures of guys leaning on the bonnets of their BMWs or Mercedes', often topless and striking a pose. This made me laugh and roll my eyes; that people could be so shallow and misguided to think that this approach would be the deal clincher.

I had always been a realist and yes, like anyone, liked the material things in life if I could afford them. But these were more of a bonus than an actual necessity. And the usual clichéd introductions were definitely not me. Some of the profiles were jaw-dropping.

I was very honest in my profile. I mean what was the point in describing a 5ft 9 inch green eyed, blonde haired, size 8-10 Jamie Lee Curtis lookalike unless you actually looked like that?

Fortunately for me I did, so my description text took very little time.

It was his picture that caught my eye. Olive skin, chunky set, 5ft 9, shaved head, boxer's nose and a smile that set his eyes on fire. He was dressed in a blue suit with a dark collared open-neck shirt, leaning back in his seat and laughing. It was a real can't breathe laugh as opposed to an insincere smile. There were other people around the table in the picture but there was something that drew my eyes to him. And those eyes. Distinctive, dark and so piercing. He was a picture of cool confidence.

'Bloody typical', I mumbled and let out a deep sigh.

He was living in Maidstone, the opposite side of the country. He described himself grammatically very well, not a spelling mistake or incorrectly used phrase in sight. I had absolutely no need to read his dialogue ten times before it made sense, which was a huge and refreshing bonus.

I hovered my finger over the *Match* button and clicked in the message box.

Hmm...what to write?

Hi there...

Delete.

Hi, love the suit...

No way, too cheesy. Delete.

Come on, just be yourself, think girl....

The good news is you are smiling because I have just liked your profile. The bad? Well, you will have to travel across the breadth of the country to sunny Wales to find me.

Click...*sending*...delivered!

Less than twenty-four hours later, the suited smiler had responded.

And so, it began.

Messaging soon progressed to real conversations. His telephone voice was deep and proper London pie 'n' mash.

Initially I chose not to reveal my occupational status as I had found it could be a right old conversation stopper. I would save that revelation for another time.

He was articulate, funny and seemingly successful with his own distribution business.

I checked everything out and it all added up. He was the genuine article and I found myself falling for him. I quite simply could not believe my luck.

Now Dean's words brought me back to the present.

'I have a few meetings at the office tonight, but it should all be done by 9-ish.'

Within a few moments of the call ending a text message beeped through. It was 19.16:

Love you, call you a bit later.

But he didn't call.

And that was not normal.

I went to bed that night and tried to call his mobile a few times but every time it diverted straight to answer phone.

I tried his other numbers. All the same.

Ah well, I thought, maybe things have run on in work and he is tied up, I will catch him tomorrow.

Tomorrow arrived: 1 November 2006.

It was a pretty regular day at work for me aside

from the nagging discomfort that the ongoing silence was creating. I messaged his mum and asked if she had heard from him but just received a bland message in return saying he was probably busy and not to worry.

But I was starting to worry. Something was not right. That was my gut feeling. The dialling tone is a very lonely sound when you are desperate for answers. By early evening, once darkness crept in, things seemed a million times worse.

Six o'clock arrived. Still nothing. The news was on the TV as I made the evening meal. With two children, there was little time to myself after a working day so it had become habit to catch up with the day's news at teatime.

It was the usual stuff, Diana v Camilla in the fashion stakes and taxpayers facing huge tax bills. Then something made me pause a second, turn up the volume and listen a little more closely.

'De Menezes family *horrified* by new police shooting. The family of Jean Charles de Menezes reacted with horror today after it has emerged that one of the police marksmen involved in his shooting has again shot and killed a forty-two-year-old man during an operation to foil an armed robbery yesterday at the Nationwide Building Society in New Romney.'

Blimey! I remembered the shooting of De Menezes in the London tube and the controversy that surrounded his death, specifically concerning the actions of the police.

How weird is that? The same officer fatally shooting a bank robber in such a short period of time? Oh well, shouldn't be robbing banks then, should you!

The second half of Coronation Street had just resumed when the silence broke. My phone beeped. At last a message:

Go to a phone box, call this number and ask for Debbie. Do not reply to this.

Debbie was Dean's sister. I had met her a number of times. Phone box? I didn't even question why a phone box or indeed anything at all, I was just desperate for an answer to the excruciating silence which was menacing and starving me of answers.

'Girls, Mummy is just popping out to get some milk,' was all the originality I could muster before I was out the door and driving down the road.

I couldn't see the phone in the box. The dirty glass had misted up from the inside with the cold air. The light inside flickered. I opened the door and was met with the overwhelming smell of urine. As I looked down, I noticed my feet were buried under a mountain of sodden dirty leaves mixed with rubbish and rotting bits of food. My hands were shaking as I pressed the 20p into the slot, punched the silver buttons and placed the grubby black receiver to my ear. Two rings and it was picked up.

'Debbie, it's Jill. What the bloody hell is going on?' Not stopping for breath, I continued.

'Two days of silence, where the hell is he, please can you tell him he needs to call tonight?'

Although it wasn't Dean's voice on the other end, the relief of the broken silence washed over me, and the contact was like a lifesaving hand.

'Jill. Stop! Dean has been involved in an incident with the police and they shot at them and one is dead.'

Silence. This time on my end.

The lifesaving hand withdrew. I gulped and fought to unstick my tongue from the roof of my suddenly desert-like mouth.

'What did you say? The words 'shot' and 'dead' bounced around the walls of my brain. I expelled them for the nonsense they were. 'Oh yes, very funny Debbie and a bit extreme if not very original. Do you think I was born yesterday? Listen you tell him if I don't get a call tonight this relationship is over.'

'Jill, please listen to me. It's all over the news, armed police have shot a man dead.'

I stopped breathing and the phone box felt like a spinning top that quickly accelerates at speed with very little effort. Suddenly the news article on De Mendez bounced back into my mind.

The armed robber shooting.

This cannot be real. This has got to be some elaborate prank, but it's not April Fools' and it makes no sense.

'Jill, are you there?'

'You're telling me Dean is dead? Shot dead? Dead? Who shot him? Why the hell would they shoot him dead?'

My voice had a nervous half laughing tone to it as I spoke with sarcasm in the hope she was going to tell me not to be so stupid. But my stomach was now churning like an over filled cement mixer and I could feel its contents starting to rise, slowly up my chest.

"No, not Dean, his mate. But Dean, his Dad and my daughter's boyfriend have been arrested and are in custody. If you don't believe me you can see it on teletext, it's all over the newspapers.'

Boom!

That was it. I couldn't think of anything to say and there was little more Debbie could have said. I was incapable of scrambling my brain into any logical thought to make it communicate with the gaping hole that had appeared where my mouth was.

What the bloody hell was he doing at an armed robbery? This was a huge mistake, a colossal mix up. It had to be.

The phone flat lined and the ensuing tone felt like I was plugged into a life-support machine which had just lost all power, yet my heart was beating so hard it was deafening me.

What the fuck have I just heard? What the fuck is going on?

I slammed the phone back on its hook like it had burned me and used my body weight to shove the door open, fling myself out on to the pavement and gulp down some fresh, ammonia-free air.

I remember cars driving past, stopping for chips at the nearby chippy and feeling jealous of the occupants having a normal evening while I stood there in limbo, head fried, trying to make sense of what I had just heard.

At the same time, I felt guilty for even having a conversation about shooting, guns and the police outside of my work environment. It was not right, and something now was very wrong.

Autopilot swung into action and somehow, I got myself home, my brain racing laps, working out how I would appear absolutely normal in front of my girls.

I managed.

I tucked the girls in and played a blinding performance of normality… on that night at least.

Once they were asleep, I pressed the buttons on the remote like my life depended on it and there, as promised, on the main news headlines ticker tape bar scrolling across the bottom of the screen: *New Romney shooting. One armed robber dead. Three in custody.*

I could hardly breathe. It dawned on me: it was bloody true.

One of the three in custody was Dean. This was not a sick joke. Dean was one of the armed robbers.

No, it's not possible, it's not true, I know him, I love him. He distributes cosmetics, he does not discharge firearms! And me. Jill Evans, police sergeant. For fuck's sake, this is as ridiculous as it gets.

My girls were asleep, safe, sound and snuggled in bed without a care in the world.

For me however, it was a different story. I started to shake and sob. There was no normality, warmth or sense of security and there was definitely no escape to sleep.

That night I did not tell anyone. Not one soul. Nobody would have guessed anyway. A few friends were aware that I was in a serious relationship with Dean but as far as they and I knew, he was a businessman of the legitimate variety, not a bloody armed robber. Nobody would have guessed that he was one of those arrested. At that stage none of the armed robbers had been named.

But surely it would only be a matter of time.

Every half hour I checked the news. I convinced myself I was in some sort of cruel nightmare and that there would of course be a time when I would be told it was all one great big misunderstanding. I convinced myself he was going to call me and resume the normality that now seemed such a long time ago.

I spent most of that long night watching the hours drag by, staring at the bulb on my bedside lamp for some sort of inspiration. I closed my eyes to try and rest the spinning top inside my head that had not ceased or slowed since I left the phone box.

Morning dawned. No change. This was real.

I knew I had to make the call.

Chief Superintendent Amphlett was my boss at that time. He headed up the Pembrokeshire Division. A lovely guy. He was approachable, friendly and honest, not the usual jobsworth ready to cut anyone's throat while climbing the greasy ladder of promotion. He was more of an 'open door man,' not everything was black and white, we were allowed to have grey areas. My grey area however was now becoming greyer by the second, almost black.

I called the office, but I could not access him directly as I had to bypass an interrogation by his PA. This particular one was very stern and had a nose like a sniffer dog. She was a large matronly woman; I would always hear her tights rubbing together on her thighs when she walked. You were lucky to get a smile even on a rare, good day.

She was also in charge of pay and overtime claims. Her desk was always full of pink overtime cards which she would scrutinise and cover in red pen like a frustrated schoolteacher.

I did not want an interrogation this morning, I wanted a quick and painless exchange.

'Is the boss in please I need to speak to him urgently?'

'Morning, I don't think he is yet, I will take a message though.'

'No, no message, can you please check his office. I need to speak to him urgently.'

She let out a deep sigh, 'Hang on, I'll check.'

I was by now getting used to being held to the mercy of the phone and heard her shoes clacking on the tiled floor towards his office. Two quick knocks followed by the monotone and faint hum of conversation, before the clacking steps returned and then the words, preceded of course by another deep sigh. 'Putting you through.'

'Hi Jill.'

I took a deep breath.

'Boss, you need to come to my house. Something awful has happened, you just need to come over now.'

'What is…?'

'Boss, just get here please.'

I could feel my voice breaking as a wave of emotion started to kick in.

'Ok, ok stay calm. Whatever has happened to warrant this?'

'Just get here I will explain.' I sobbed.

'Okay, okay, I'm leaving now.'

Chief Superintendent Amphlett was a tall, slim and

anaemic looking man, stood on the doorstep wearing his hat and tunic. But this was no trick or treat replay. He was so pale he looked like he needed a good holiday or a good spray tan, I wasn't really sure which.

He stepped inside my living room whilst I composed myself. I had to put into words what I was struggling to comprehend myself. But the tears had started, and the emotion was clouding my already incoherent thought processes.

He stepped forward to comfort me but in a very awkward manner, robotically patting my shoulder in sympathy, obviously guarded of his position and rank yet clearly torn between that and basic human compassion.

I wiped my eyes and restored some vision and he sat down.

'Okay, so, my partner, Dean Jenkins...' I could hardly force the words out, '... you don't know him, but he is the father of my unborn child...'

He smiled slightly, 'What about him?'

'He's been arrested for armed robbery.'

He shuffled forward on the sofa. 'I beg your pardon?'

'The Building Society in Herne Bay on Halloween. He's been arrested.'

'What are you talking about?'

'One of the gang members has been shot dead,' I blurted out between the tears, 'the other two are under arrest and in custody, one of them is Dean's father, the other his niece's boyfriend.'

Silence.

What little colour he had in his face drained, leaving his skin looking like crepe paper.

'I didn't know what to do Boss. I'm telling you so you can tell Kent Police it's nothing to do with me.'

I could hear my words, they sounded weak and pathetic, almost childlike as if trying to justify my innocence for something I hadn't even done.

The silence was now deafening. He looked around the room as if he didn't want to make eye contact with me.

'Sir, I didn't know. I've only just found out. Please, you need to help me.'

A long exhale of breath through his nose before he opened his mouth.

Then just a single word.

'Jesus.'

2

A Girl in Blue

I joined Dyfed Powys Police on 17 September 1990.

I had not long completed an English degree followed by a glorious year at Swansea University completing my postgraduate teaching qualification, giving me the grand title of B.A (Hons) B.Ed. I was twenty-three years old and my parents had high hopes of me becoming an English teacher. I would be able to write these qualifications behind my name and impress anyone I had the pleasure to meet. But I had other ideas. My qualifications were my achievements and not something to wave in anyone's face. There was more to me than that. The police was something I had set my heart on.

I'm not sure whether this desire was the influence of *The Bill*, a popular television police drama series which I would avidly watch growing up. Or maybe the Inspector Clouseau films that had me looking in the mirror side-eyeing my reflection while wearing my dad's trilby hat and visualising my adult career. Either way, the whole idea would have been additionally fuelled by the fact that I was, at the time, engaged to a serving officer who had been a childhood sweetheart.

Up to this point, although having been to college, I was not worldly-wise, having only worked to fund my social life in the local Wimpy, grilling burgers and later as a promotional girl for Wickes Building Supplies. This was one giant step into the adult world of real work which I had to take seriously.

The selection process for the police was pretty intense and following the written application was a marked exam which basically tested my ability to write, calculate maths and correctly answer general knowledge questions. Having passed this with relative ease I then progressed to the two-day extended interview process.

Here the delights multiplied tenfold as this was a residential course held at Carmarthen where I stayed overnight with nine other hopeful recruits. All were of various ages, gender and background with one common goal: To pass the two-day assessment.

Throughout this forty-eight-hour window I was under continuous observation participating in classroom-based scenarios and team problem-solving tasks that tested leadership, communication, empathy and interaction with others, to name but a few. These were the basic skills required to show potential as a then, prospective, policewoman.

During the first evening we were invited to the on-site police bar, which was quite a clever move as it was obvious to me, but maybe not all, that the group was still being monitored. It wasn't rocket science as the assessors joined us under the guise of simply being social. I have never been a drinker. In fact, one wine was and still is enough to set my head spinning but I figured that if I declined to participate it would indirectly be construed as not being a team player. That was not a risk I was prepared to take.

This is where a few of the candidates made terminal errors of judgement and downed pints of beer as if it was another task to drink the bar dry. I am unsure whether they simply did not register the reality of why the assessment team was there or whether it was simply a release from what had been a stressful and relatively intense day.

As the night wore slowly on, so did the increasing volume in both beer and noise. One candidate stood up on the plush red velvet bench, gyrating his hips while holding his pint in the air like some kind of trophy he had received for making it through day one. This trophy wasn't aloft for long as he lurched forward and came crashing down on the table in front of us, sending drinks and glasses in all directions.

Funny for others maybe but unfortunately for him the end of his selection process as come 9am the following morning with fitness test looming, he and his newly bonded comrades were missing from the gym. Indeed they had left the building.

The group of ten was down to seven.

So, having completed one day of mental pressure, the next thing on the list was physical fitness. At that time and throughout all of my training this was key; you would not find unfit recruits and failure to meet the required standard at any point would, without question, mean being sent to join a more junior course until you could raise your game or be dismissed.

The first fitness test was a mile and a half run in thirteen minutes or under. I remember it was a cold, frosty but sunny morning and I had bought a new pair of purple running shorts especially for the occasion just to look the part and show keen. The route was out of headquarters up a long and steady hill to the top where I had to double back down a farm road with a decline gradient as far as an old oak tree, turn around and get back into HQ before the clock hit thirteen minutes.

Stupidly I didn't wear a watch, but I didn't need it

as the resident PTI boomed the times out as he ran with us. Coming back down that hill my legs became ostrich-like as my mind was by this stage playing tricks, convincing me I was out of time after all that effort. The PTI at this juncture had long returned to the finish line, standing with the stopwatch of doom, like the gatekeeper of the finish line. On this occasion it ticked in my favour and, despite the air burning my throat as it made its way down to fuel my thumping heart and legs which stung with the coldness of the wind, I found a final sprint finish to pass the line at around the 11 minute mark.

Two failed this particular event. One in tears and the other arguing the timings with the PTI. This was futile. He took no shit and both were homeward bound.

Seven became five.

Back inside to the welcoming warmth of the gymnasium, the tests continued.

Press-ups, sit-ups, flexibility (push a bar as far forward as possible while sat down with straight legs, feet against a box, leaning forward to push the gauge), grip strength test and then finally body fat percentage for age and gender.

The final afternoon session involved me showered and back in a suit for an intense interview with a Chief Inspector. My fate was delivered.

I had passed with flying colours. Delighted was an understatement. I recall driving down the A40 towards home beaming with pride and the sort of excitement that made me randomly shriek aloud and furiously shake my legs like I was swimming. I had done it and would commence basic training on 17 September 1990 at Police Headquarters with the rest of course intake, known as 09/90.

In the classroom that day, in my purple knee-length pencil skirt and blouse (I think purple must have been the colour of the time), I sat alongside eight male colleagues. I was the only female on the course, which says a lot about the gender gap prevalent in recruitment during that period. This of course may have fazed a lot of people but to me it felt absolutely normal, having always preferred to be in the company of men. I found them less complicated and far less headwork than a gaggle of gossiping women.

I was issued with my uniform which was different to my male colleagues. I had a skirt while the men were issued trousers. I also had a handbag and for me, not a handbag person, this was simply more of a hindrance than a help, although it did come complete with truncheon holder attached. My wooden truncheon was the smallest I had ever set eyes on. The men however were blessed with a full-size version. It was no surprise when one of my colleagues got hold of mine and brutally engraved the end to resemble a penis. As these truncheons were not replaceable, that was how it was to remain.

I dare not say a word and in its holder it stayed. Thankfully progress saw it replaced with a baton where one size fits all and uniform became more universal as opposed to gender dictated.

Throughout my training, which at that time was split between Carmarthen Police headquarters and Cwmbran, I was always expected to do the same as my colleagues. There were absolutely no allowances made, not that I expected there to be. Cwmbran was a residential course where I spent months mixed with colleagues from other forces as it was a national police training facility. If I had any hopes, which of course I didn't, of getting off more lightly than my male colleagues because I was a woman, then I would have been in for a large wake-up call.

One day on the Parade square we had to practice drill marching. The drill sergeant who was ex forces had the loudest voice and the discipline to match.

He was immaculately presented. Pristine creased black uniform, the boots and peak of his hat so shiny you could see your face in them. He walked with such authority and purpose you just held your breath in case simply breathing sparked an onslaught of public verbal abuse.

Drill practice involved marching with the other course recruits. Back and forth we stomped in all kinds of weather, our goal to pass out from college in some sort of professional semblance. The pass-out parade took place in front of friends and family and there was no room or excuse, as reminded daily, for looking like a sack of shit. Uniform had to be pristine. Two creases in the skirts both front and back, leather shoes so dazzling and polished they looked nothing less than patent and not one speck of dust on the tunic otherwise it was curtains. Like it or not, it certainly taught me discipline, attention to detail and a habit of taking a pride in my appearance.

Many recruits simply could not march in correct time and would resemble what I can only describe as 'tick tock' soldiers which looked hilarious especially when accompanied by the look of concentration on their faces. Never had so many people wished their bodies would just simply do what this drill sergeant bellowed as he did not see the funny side. The 'tick-tockers' did have a purpose, simply to re-ignite the fuse of his wrath.

There was one WPC (woman police constable, a title long obsolete) called Charlene who was not what I would describe as being blessed with supermodel looks and, in the brutal climate we were in, this was obviously picked up on by the males on camp, including the drill sergeant.

'So, you miserable lot.'

'Click...click...click' was the only sound, it came from his boots on the concrete

'We will be marching around this fucking square on the day your families come to watch your shower of shit, in the same order that we practice in. Is that fucking clear?'

Silence.

I was at this stage lined up and stood to attention in the front line of around eight rows with the drill sergeant pacing up and down in front of us. The peak of his cap was pulled down over his eyes so low that all you could see was his nose sticking out like a beak. His lips moving and his booming voice echoing across the great acoustics of the parade square. His gait and manner reminded me of an ostrich, long sure-footed strides but if something caught his attention, he could cover at least sixteen feet it seemed in just one. He gripped his long pace stick like a weapon as he eyed and dared each of our faces to move.

He continued. 'That is unless the weather becomes in-clement and for those of the more stupid amongst you that does not mean we will be marching inside fucking St Clements's church down the road!'

The silence then suddenly broke, like a river bursting its banks, but not all the water was escaping, the initial trickle was one of laughter screeching from Charlene's mouth, a cackle of a laugh which echoed around the whole square.

Oh, God.

The drill sergeant erupted like a volcano; his booming voice bounced off all four surrounding walls. The ostrich was off and hotfooting it in her direction.

'What the fuck do we have here?' The beak looked her up and down. 'I suggest you shut that fucking great gob of yours and get a grip of yourself you bloody mess!' He screamed the words, standing almost beak to nose, little more than an inch away from her face. 'Otherwise I will be shoving this pace stick where something has clearly not been shoved for a very long time.'

The overwhelming urge to laugh was so painful and I remember an awkward universal shuffle ripple through the lines, like a silent but powerful wave. I just prayed for practice to be over.

Charlene however voiced no complaint of bullying or inappropriate behaviour with regard to this incident. I don't believe she even viewed it as that. She laughed as hard as the rest of us did once it was safe to do so. We were there training in a disciplined environment for a career we all desperately wanted to succeed in and rocking any unnecessary boats, let alone the one being steered by captain Beaky, was not on the agenda. Life was hard enough as it was.

I accepted this behaviour as normal. In some respects, it was subconsciously flattering that to be on the end of it meant I was accepted as one of the team. From the training-staff point of view it proved that you would be able to withstand a verbal battering without reaction. This was important, as far worse would be faced on the streets.

Now don't get me wrong, everyone is different and

there were some women who constantly strove and were on a mission to prove they were stronger and better than their male colleagues. This kind attitude had the opposite effect to what I suppose was the desired goal. They lost the respect of colleagues around them and were viewed more of a nuisance with a constant point to prove. I didn't subscribe to this concept, simply because I did not think it was possible to be physically stronger than the boys and regardless, why would I want to be? I had nothing to prove to anyone other than myself.

I have always been one to do the best I can in whatever circumstances are thrown at me. If I was fitter than some male colleagues then so be it. If I couldn't lift something but they could, I was bloody grateful for them to take over. If I wasn't selected to do a task because a male was more suitable and the reasoning was explained, I got it and thoughts of objection on any grounds, at that time, never crossed my mind.

I am not sure whether that was due to a lack of confidence, immaturity in my new role and the desire to comply, or whether it was simply the culture at that time, which didn't flag up as being a problem. Or maybe a bit of both.

What it boiled down to for me was in a world dominated by male officers, I liked being a woman. I was happy with my gender and although I knew my life, what would be and was expected of me, was changing, I did not want to lose my femininity or become one of the lads *per se*. I just wanted to slot in and fulfil my role without fuss.

However, there was another side to being in the minority gender in such a closed environment.

And that was relationships.

It did not matter whether married, single or happily spoken for, nobody was spared and even some of the strongest individuals found themselves in tears as they found new love, or at last what they perceived as love. To many of the married male officers it was nothing more than extramarital sex, a close and convenient mistress.

Instructors formed fleeting physical relationships with students and rumour had it that a few students fell pregnant as a result. People easily became besotted with others as we lived, breathed, studied, and ate together daily. Those left back home, none the wiser to the actualities of the training and the bonds that were built, inevitably would find themselves as a preferred second choice.

For example, my fiancé obviously could not see in the same way how funny an incident was that I excitedly recounted to him, as he needed to be there at the time. I would view his lack of reaction as a lack of support. Although he had been through it and understood how it went as a serving officer himself, we found ourselves drifting apart.

3

40

I had struck up a close friendship with a fellow course member, commonly known as '40' as per his collar number. He eventually succumbed to the same fate as many in that his wife apparently 'did not understand him and the marriage was over'. This was a clichéd turn of phrase, I suppose to justify the guilt of infidelity which became more of a common excuse as I watched many relationships, including my own, fail.

We had an instant connection on that first day in Carmarthen. I wasn't looking for a relationship, but I had been thrown in the deep end with an unexpected all male group and wanted to feel at ease and also accepted by them. He, like the rest, was supportive from the start and we quickly bonded as a group, working together all day and socialising at night in the very same bar where selection had been held. Ironically, in the first week, I was the one who drank too many wines although I didn't quite dance on the tables and was safely put to bed by the group after a detour to the block toilets. There was no funny business and I was treated with the same respect and trust as they treated each other hence the swiftly developed bond between us all. But there was something different with 40. I could just sense it and it was confirmed one night when the group decided to chip in for a takeaway to be collected and brought back to HQ. As I was the most useless drinker, I simply avoided drink so naturally volunteered to be the one to drive and fetch it .40 volunteered himself to ride shotgun and used the more private setting of my red Fiat Uno Turbo sport to make an important announcement.

'Have you got the same excited feeling as me?' he announced as I bundled the brown paper bags full of burgers across the steering wheel from the drive through window.

'Oh God yes, I love a good burger it will make a change from the food back in HQ.'

I looked at his half hidden face behind the fence of straws sticking out from the milk shake cups he was juggling in his large, shovel hands.

'Not the food doll, I'm talking about us?'

I gripped the suede leather steering wheel and involuntarily traced my thumb over the raised red sport stitching. My feelings were leaking out of me like a dripping tap. My heart thumped in my ears.

I parked the car and we both grinned in the electric silence, his face part illuminated by the orange glow from the dashboard.

'I know what you are thinking, I'm married. But it's not a happy marriage and it won't last. There was something about you the first day you walked into that classroom.'

I took a deep breath and could hear the nervousness in my voice.

'You are right, there is something here but there are also people to hurt. My fiancé at home for starters.'

Nick was a childhood sweetheart. I genuinely loved him but was realistically not ready to settle down. And these feelings should not have been there if I was truly happy.

I leaned across and planted a kiss on the lips of burger laden 40. I looked at him and released a deep sigh that fanned the white serviettes on top of the milkshake cups, as if they were fanning the flames of that passion fuelled revelation between us. I looked into his smiling eyes and spoke calmly.

'Let's get this food inside before this heat melts the shakes.'

As I lay in my block accommodation bed that night I knew I would have to be honest and end my current chapter before starting a new one. Hiding my feelings is a near on impossibility for me and I figured although painful, honesty was the least stressful option.

That weekend I sat down with Nick and discussed our relationship .His agreement that it was the correct thing to do for both our sakes, confirmed that our relationship had run its course. There were no tears and no animosity. It was the simplest and most adult ending to a relationship and my memories of Nick have never been anything but good ones.

As the closeness with 40 grew, I wanted to be at work 24/7. Home life seemed boring in contrast. In my world nobody understood the training I was going through like 40 did. It got to a point where that closeness became all-consuming. We ate, worked and socialised together and the progression to a physical relationship was inevitable.

It happened one weekend in Cwmbran. Instead of travelling home he made some excuse to his wife that the whole course had to stay over because of a policing exercise. It did remain open for students to stay if needed and events did occur there on weekends. We chose one such weekend so had anyone called the centre it would have checked out.

We didn't travel far. Travelodges were in abundance, a novelty and most importantly, cheap.

As I walked through to reception at Cardiff Services (it had to be me in case he was seen), a young girl was sat at the desk, painting her fingernails.

'Hello, do you have a reservation?'

'Hi...Uhm...no I don't, sorry. I'm looking for a double room?'

She looked up and smiled

I was embarrassed. She knew what was happening.

'Oh yes, Madam, just for you?' She was grinning. Smugly.

I cringed. She damn well knew it wasn't just for me. Did she really have to say it so loudly?

Customers were now trickling in behind me and I found myself thinking, ridiculously, that one must surely be his wife, so I dare not look around. I felt like a rabbit in the headlights.

'Uhm, no, for myself and my...'

My *what*, I thought. What the hell was he? Lover to be? Ha-ha, no, I couldn't say that.

'Boyfriend. Yes, my boyfriend.'

'Ah, I see!' She winked and nodded her head.

I bet she did.

'Cash or card payment?'

'Cash please.' No way am I using a card with my name on it.

I handed over the money and the deal, thank God, was done.

Had I been older, this exchange would have been

handled with far more confidence. But I was young and petrified of being rumbled. My guilty feelings added to this and I gave everything away with my body language and panic. I didn't need the help of anyone else.

'Room 10, second floor, up the stairs and turn left. Please sign here Mrs Smith.'

I was so original!

Paperwork done and small key on a giant white key fob in hand I returned to the black Capri where he was peering out as if on a stake-out.

Regardless I was jubilant, waving the key about in triumph.

It wasn't the most romantic of settings, TV on and a service station takeaway burger. But for that one evening it was just us. We could pretend that for one night we were a straightforward, regular couple. It was perfect. The excitement off the scale, raw hungry and forbidden passion made it all the more dangerously inviting.

After this night, the relationship was cemented, and our attachment grew.

Travelodge group at locations up and down the M4 did well out of us both that year.

Thus, friendship morphed to intimacy and I was a free agent. He, however, remained married and things were not simple.

We would see each other daily at Cwmbran. There

were no mobile phones then and communication was through letters, as even the residential blocks were split into gender and never the twain should meet. If you were caught in the wrong block there would be trouble, and nobody wanted to be sent back to force for such an embarrassing reason. The antics of the brave however were well documented, stories of people hiding under the cast iron beds when caught on the hop during an impromptu room inspection.

On one occasion we had had a thick dumping of snow and one of the male recruits had been in the female block having an intimate liaison in one of the rooms. As I recall the story, after the deed was done, while he was lying in the bed, she opened the wardrobe and pulled out a wedding dress casually explaining it had been on the sale and she was thinking ahead for the wedding. The problem was, they were not engaged and there was a slight technicality in that he was already 'happily' married. This live revelation was further electrified with the sound of a booming voice emanating from the corridor below.

'Inspection!'

He leaped from the bed and the only option was the first-floor window, in his pants. *Pants* were emphasised in the recounting of this story in the bar later that night, not boxers, which somehow made it all funnier. He crash-landed in the snow below in his grey waist high Y-fronts. He never did get identified and the relationship seemed to melt faster than the snow that had saved him a few broken bones and a trip back to Force.

We were all in different classes at Cwmbran as the policy was to mix up the different force recruits to facilitate integration. Each day on the way to class we would have to walk in full uniform, tunic and hat, along the cloisters and into the building. Our tunics displayed our collar number and these were to be hung in the cloak room to be collected at the end of the day. I would often retrieve mine to find a letter from 40 in the pocket, which fuelled the romantic fire. He played for Swansea Rugby club at that time and I would often go with him and others for a spin in his black Ford Capri on a Thursday night to watch him train. We would sneak contact by holding hands down the side of the car seat if I had managed to bag the seat behind him.

We also went for early morning runs and 'casually' bumped into each other. We would travel home in convoy after a long week, stop for lunch together and he would always pull in before his turn-off, get out of the car and give me a kiss. A kiss of frustration often accompanied by a deep sigh as if in battle with himself with the burden of returning home and hiding the affair and leaving me for the weekend.

The less romantic reality? Pure guilt.

It was common knowledge there was something

going on between us but the habit of sneaking around and denying all suggestions of being anything other than close friends, remained in place regardless of where we were. I would imagine this was to the amusement of many who could see what was more than blatantly obvious.

But there were other policing skills to be mastered.

My first posting was Newtown. I vividly recall the tutor constable I was assigned to until I was deemed competent to work alone or at least, independently.

Sledge as he was known, was a tall, slight man with thick Welsh drawl and had a mop of black hair which resembled being cut around a pudding bowl, giving him the roundest of fringes. He wore boots where the fronts were so round, they looked like they were borrowed from a clown. He was happily married with two children. All in all, he was a thoroughly nice guy and he taught me the hard way and, I feel, the best way.

Night shift would see us plodding the streets of Newtown, checking door handles of shops, freezing noses pressed up against windows peering into the darkness to make sure no burglars were at work. I walked in all weather, frozen to the bone until around 5am when I would head back to station after six hours of pounding deserted streets. Those nights were long ones but a solid foundation.

There was a lingerie shop on the High Street, lit up like a Christmas tree and we plodded past it during most night shifts, my tutor peering in of course nose squashed against the glass to check for intruders and then immediately giving the game away as to the real reason for the length of time we paused there.

'Well now…umm…Jill baaacchh …what do you…umm…think of that now…umm…I bet you are wearing something like that under that lot,' nodding his head in a downward motion at my outdoor apparel. I had piled on everything I could find ready for these Baltic walks, even borrowing an old-fashioned black police woollen cape to stave off the inevitable hypothermia. I could barely be seen, my frame swamped by the layers with just my eyes peeking out, like the black ninja.

In fact, underneath my M&S knickers and matching thermals, I bore more resemblance to a heavily bandaged mummy, the complete unsexy opposite to the lacy suspendered vision brightening up my tutor's midnight stroll. I recall us laughing in tandem, comfortable in each other's presence and both aware that his words couldn't be further from the truth.

I hated the cold, so a run of seven-night walks in freezing Newtown was never my favourite shift unless I managed to be attached to the traffic car when my tutor was away. I would happily and thankfully jump into the old Rover 827, the traffic vehicle at the time. 827 was my collar number too. I recall the comments as regular as clockwork 'Can't wait to get inside the 827, bet it's nice and warm in there.' These remarks were commonplace, but I always accepted them as banter with no offence meant. It was life in the police service and to make a fuss or to react would raise questions as to how suited you actually were to that job. More importantly, you would not be 'one of the boys'. My final acceptance into this club involved being placed headfirst into a tall wheelie bin to establish whether I wore regulation underwear. Of course, I did not, no such thing existed. Once that was established without complaint, I became a fully accepted and trusted shift member.

There was a female sergeant at the station. Just one. Females of rank were, at that time, an exception rather than rule. She was tall, slim and very smart with grey hair but, I felt, not the most welcoming. I quickly learned she had set herself up as the station matriarch. She definitely wasn't a candidate for a bin insertion or any form of knicker inspection, but she liked to cluck around the men and be the mother hen. She did not take me under her wing and in some respects, I think she viewed me as more of an inconvenience and not a great addition to the brood.

Policewomen can be strange beings. I think there is a lot of jealousy and, in this situation, a new face on the block, taking the attention away from the mothership, was inevitably going to cause friction.

One particular shift, shortly after my arrival, I was

allocated station duties which involved dealing with customers at the front desk and answering the phones. A phone call came in to which I didn't have a clue how to respond. Respect for rank was obviously very important in those days and you would address by rank as opposed to name, unless you had known that person for years when it no longer became viewed as disrespectful to address on first name terms.

Everybody was busy in the control room and I answered the incoming call as professionally as I could muster, hoping that the caller would not detect that I had five minutes experience in the job and didn't have a clue what the hell I was doing. The phone receiver felt like it was burning in my hand. The customer was waiting for a response to her question and I was clueless as to what to say… I just didn't know… so I panicked and covering the phone with my hand, shouted 'Gloria, can you help me please?'

Silence.

It was like the control room had suddenly become that pub from a scene in *An American Werewolf in London*. Everyone turned silently and watched. I had committed the most unforgivable sin. I had not referred to her as 'Sergeant'.

She never really did seem to warm to me following that, but it didn't really matter anyway. I learned a memorable lesson in respect of addressing rank which I never forgot. I did not repeat the mistake.

4

Kindred Spirits

I completed my two-year probationary period and was packed off on summer posting to Tenby, Pembrokeshire. The posting later became permanent.

Tenby was a seaside station with the same ethics but different people. It was far more relaxed, although maybe I felt this as I was growing in confidence, had passed the probationary milestone and had a tiny bit of credibility.

My sergeant there was Sergeant Hamblin. He was just the best. Such a funny down to earth man, always wearing thick rimmed glasses, tall with a mop of dark hair. At times he looked like he had just rolled in out of bed and always had a cigarette in one hand. He loved to fish, and his skin was tanned as a result. He spent most of his life in the station even when off duty, surrounded by a plume of cigarette smoke.

The station was like a second home and many would pop in there when not on shift. It was a nice place to be.

I noticed a slight movement in my perspective as my confidence and ability to do the job began to grow.

Prisoner escort duties were like gold dust and when they did come around it was a cock fight to be on them. Basically, in the days before the police escort company Serco, collecting and transporting 'wanted' prisoners was down individual Forces. Everyone wanted to go on escort as it meant an easy shift and they almost always incurred overtime.

One day a prisoner needed escorting to Gloucester prison. Sergeant Hamblin used to allocate this on a rota system so we would all get an equal share of escort duties. Today was my day.

'No not your day today Jill, this guy is a nutter and if he kicks off in the car, I will need men there. It's not a woman's job, you can have the next one. I'm gasping for a brew, put the kettle on.' And with that he disappeared in a plume of smoke.

That was the first time I felt irritated by the perception of my sex being used as a hindrance in my job. Had he stopped after 'there', I would have accepted his words, it was just the remainder of the sentence that grated on me as I stood, open-mouthed.

I was furious, so much so that I bypassed the kettle, stormed up to my police flat located within the grounds of the station, and remained there for at least two hours, properly sulking with rage.

Once I had calmed down, I returned to the office where he simply looked at me, smiled and drew slowly on his cigarette. He spoke calmly. 'That brew is taking its time.'

Aargh! How could I hate him?

I smiled and headed to the tearoom.

Times were a-changing and that was my first experience of what I felt was discrimination, which was hard for those old-school officers to understand. It certainly wasn't deliberate. I don't believe that many like Sergeant Hamblin had any intention of causing offence. It was simply that culture was evolving faster than they could keep up with and, in practical terms, he genuinely felt two men would be the safer option while simultaneously looking after me.

It was while stationed at Tenby that I met my first husband, David.

My personal life was not settled. I was wrapped up with the on / off encounters with 40, who unwrapped me whenever he got the opportunity, but never offered the commitment I was looking for. Or the promised divorce papers. It came to a point where I started wondering where my life was heading.

I was posted back to Haverfordwest, my hometown, where at twenty-six years old, my thoughts started to move towards children, although career progression was always a big part of my long-term plans.

David moved back home to Pembrokeshire having been stationed in Llanelli some 50 miles away. As a traffic officer he would patrol all of the Pembrokeshire roads as opposed to being stationed at one town or village. One of these roads led to Tenby where we met.

He was a tall, stocky guy who rode a motorbike like he stole it. He was a police motorcyclist and owned a GSXR 750 as well as a red Ford XR2, the car of the day. Superficially we were well matched as I was never interested in the usual 'girly' interests of hair and makeup. I found cars and motorbikes far more interesting which resulted in me always owning various sports cars and eventually passing my bike test. In the days of courting we did have a lot of fun and I remember, while riding pillion, that I often tried to cover the number plate on the bike with my hands to avoid any unnecessary tickets or complaints coming his way.

He lived at home with his parents and after six months of dating we moved in together. It made absolute sense as I was vacating my Tenby flat and also seemed a natural progression for us.

I can't say I ever had butterflies with David. He was a nice, dependable and solid guy but he was a police officer to the core and as time passed, he morphed into someone that said yes to everything without questioning the thinking of senior management.

I remember when I was expecting our daughter Ella her due dates coincided with an event called The County Show, a well-known and popular annual three-day agricultural show held in Pembrokeshire. David would always be required to work this as the bikes were obviously far more efficient for traffic management than cars. He was desperately worried that my giving birth at this time would affect the whole logistical operation if he were not there as opposed to supporting me in the birth of our first child. His loyalty and dependability to the job was unquestionable.

We ended up working in the same station in Haverfordwest as the Pembrokeshire traffic fleet were based there. It was not too much of a problem at that time as we both knew what being part of a police family was about. The grittier problem that became apparent was that he and I operated on different wavelengths. David would never take chances and always thought and operated in police mode whether on or off duty. Procedure had to be followed and there were no grey areas, whereas I held a different viewpoint that an element of common sense had to prevail. In all the time I served as an officer I am proud to say that I never lost that perspective as sometimes the expression 'the law is an ass' is very true when applied to real-life situations.

There was one occasion when he pulled up, on his way to work, at the local petrol station. Some guy whom he had previously booked was parked at the pump in front and obviously harboured a grievance towards David. As he was filling his car with fuel this guy jumped back on his motorbike and slowly manoeuvred it backwards and deliberately into the bumper of David's car. Ever conscious of doing the right thing, David's response was, 'I will see you when I'm in work'. That was David. No reaction and definitely no response that would put his job in jeopardy or risk a complaint coming his way.

This may indeed have been the better way but if it were me the guy would have been tied around the petrol pump; nozzle inserted firmly up his backside. There he would have remained until the police carted him away.

Off duty, David would often guestimate the speed cars were doing while I, rolling my eyes, would regularly confuse the rev counter for the speedometer.

We were very different.

Those differences eventually became a game changer. Whenever I was involved in incidents, I always felt there was no support from him, whether positive or negative.

I was once commended with a bravery award for saving a suicidal man from jumping off a bridge. The award involved a visit with others to tea at 10 Downing Street. I was in Bramshill College of law at this time, completing my studies to be a police law trainer. David got so drunk at that event he was sick all down the curtains in the hotel. It felt like he was deliberately trying to spoil the day and obviously caused great upset between us.

On reflection, I don't think there was anything more to it other than he had become overwhelmed with the free bar and just filled his boots, literally, forgetting the reason we were there in the first place.

At the ceremony I made a point of getting a picture with Prime Minister Tony Blair who was milling around the garden surrounded by his entourage of security. That did not faze or deter me as I squeezed my way through and introduced myself. I simply wanted a picture. David was mortified by my actions, even though I got my picture, and questioned me as to why I couldn't be 'normal' and just blend in like the rest. But I never wanted to blend in, I wanted to make the most of all opportunities or challenges heading my way.

Maybe this was an inadvertent reaction by him because he saw me first and foremost as a police officer. I just wanted him to be my husband. I felt I lacked the support and reassurance that should have been there, he instead presuming I could look after myself. I also had aspirations to use my brain and climb the ranks whereas he was just happy to sit and complete his thirty years. We were poles apart when we actually drilled down to the realities of our relationship.

His mother wasn't far off the mark in thinking we were unsuited, she hated me on sight and was overheard saying as much in the cubicle of the ladies' toilet at our wedding.

As time passed things inevitably and steadily went downhill from there. Irritation became resentment. David was fully backed by his mother and he would defend her, maybe understandably, to the last, regardless of circumstance. I felt left out on a limb as there was no compromise. I recall the time his mother drank the dog's anal ointment, mistaking it for her own medicine. I was the only one who found this quite amusing but of course this was typical, as I was told, of how apparent my 'hard and insensitive character' had become. The problem was perceived to lie with me.

Another more poignant and vivid memory was giving birth to Ella. I had a forty-eight-hour labour and was exhausted in the latter stages as she became stuck. While obviously coping with distress and exhaustion, David whispered reassuringly in my ear, 'I think you are dying'.

Fortunately, I did not die and she arrived safely. I

later collapsed in the hospital bathroom, attempting to have a bath on my own, while David chose to remain on the ward.

As the years passed, cracks became craters and I was unsurprisingly drawn back to 40.

He and I were, for a while at least, kindred spirits. We were both unhappily married but never on the same page or even line; when I was single, he was married and *vice versa*. Now, my heart would define him as my first love, but my head would contest that and say I was in love with the person I thought he was, simply desperately needed and wanted him to be. He reminded me of the Bruce type, both Willis and Forsyth. He was tall, muscular, thick set with a shaved head, a proper man's man. His sense of humour was still like a breath of fresh air and laughter with him was therapeutic, wholesome and addictive. He was an exciting escape, albeit temporarily, from the pressures of reality at that time. I felt he loved me and that was a big Brucey bonus.

We had a connection which spanned the best part of seventeen years and which eventually, despite everything, became a solid and genuine friendship. At this point in my teetering marriage to David, the affair resulted in an unexpected pregnancy. This saw 40 run faster than anyone in a *Die Hard* movie.

I remember the initial phone call I made to break

the news to him. I was in a private side office in the police station.

'Hey, remember the conversation we had about contraception, children and the fact you cannot father any?'

'Yes, I've always wanted a rugby team but unfortunately that cannot happen.'

'Well, whoever told you that is wrong, you've scored a try. I've done a pregnancy test and it's positive.'

Long silence.

'Hello? Are you still there?' The silence was making me uneasy.

'What do you mean you're pregnant?'

There was a colder tone to his voice now.

'Yes Ian that is what I am telling you. I know the timing of this is not good, but it is good news, right?'

To be honest I was looking for some hint of support from him at this time as although this was something we had not planned, I had no reason to disbelieve his infertility story. Contraception had not been a priority.

'Fuck's sake Jill!' Followed by a sigh that lasted a few long seconds. He was not at all happy and swiftly reverted to practicalities.

'We need to meet up. I will meet you in Leekes Car Park, Cross Hands, at 10am tomorrow. Right then, I've got to go.'

And he was gone, leaving me feeling like an

unnecessary burden as opposed to the soulmate he had professed to have been so lucky to have found.

However, 10am the next morning found me dutifully parked alongside him in the specified car park. It was an hour's drive for me, ten minutes for him. He jumped into the passenger seat of my grey Astra GTE and with a tentative hug, told me to drive towards the Gower coast where we eventually parked in a more private spot. He looked at me, his voice cold.

'Are you fucking serious?'

'Ian, I think I would have a pretty sick sense of humour to make something like this up, don't you?'

'Well, it can't be mine can it?'

How dare he?

I could feel the anger rise from my stomach. I fully appreciated I was having an affair behind my husband's back which I wasn't proud of, but to suggest I was engaged in a physical relationship with both at the same time was just the biggest slap in the face. I had not had any sort of relationship with David, let alone physical, for months. For me it was simple. I had fallen for 40 which meant with my loyalty was with him despite being married to someone else. The fact that he could even question that spoke volumes about his level of reciprocated allegiance to me.

'Right then.'

40 had a habit of using these words whenever he

was leaving or about to end a conversation and I knew what came next signalled the end of the meeting. By this time, we had got out of the car and were looking out over the Swansea bay. The view was beautiful and breath-takingly romantic. Unlike the words that came next in a lowered, icy voice.

'If you think I'm going to play happy families with you then you can think again. I can't even have children.'

After all the promises and previous demonstrations of love, these words hit me like a train. Nice. Touching. Classy. With the added sting of degradation that he was not the father and was one of many candidates.

Surprising words, considering that later in his life he apparently did turn out to be something of a medical wonder, miraculously fathering at least four that I know of.

The first thought to cross my mind was to get back in my car and leave him stranded. I wish that I had done. Instead, numb and empty, and trying to do the right thing I gave him a lift back to his car. We drove in silence. His words had apparently exonerated him from all responsibility and the music was mine to face alone. I felt guilty and responsible for us being in the position we were in, but especially for clearly upsetting him.

I made the long drive home.

The best decision to take was one which would save everyone else embarrassment. Termination. I considered hiding it all from David, but I felt I had done him wrong. That meant facing the consequences of what I, even though it was we, had done. I wasn't proud of myself, but I knew honesty was the best policy, even though our marriage was over.

I arrived home and not being one to be able to hide things well, came straight out with it. I put my keys on the table and sat opposite him in the living room, still wearing my coat.

'I've something to tell you.'

He fixed his eyes on me while slowly sipping his mug of tea.

Take a deep breath, I told myself.

'I've been having an affair and I am pregnant.'

David just looked at me and pushed his silver rim glasses up his nose with his hand. He placed the mug slowly down on the coffee table.

'And before you say anything, he doesn't want to know so I have no choice but to have a termination. You deserve to know, and I deserve to suffer for what I have done.'

David didn't really react to the news, the minutes were filled with my voice trying to spill out as fast as possible what had happened, without justification but simply more to get it out and release some pressure in my head.

When silence came, he spoke.

'Do I know him?'

'Yes, it's 40. But it's over now so you don't need to consider telling his wife.'

And there I was, ever loyal to the last. Still trying to look out for 40 despite being shipwrecked in my own world.

My local doctor was one who had known me since I was a child. He lived just up the road from my parents' house. The Doctor's Surgery was exactly that, one surgery with one doctor. Not the healthcare centres that exist today. The approach was far more personal. Having explained my predicament to him with the assistance of half a box of rough white surgery tissues he suggested I could have the termination done at the local hospital as the pregnancy was under twelve weeks.

This was seemingly good news, but the reality was, in my heart, I did not want the termination.

The day arrived and Jenny, my long-term friend, accompanied me to the ward of the local hospital where we were allocated a side room. The nurse was lovely and smiling sympathetically. She explained clearly that I would take two tablets and would likely feel intense period-like pains before passing the embryo into the toilet.

Taking those tablets was like willingly drinking from a poisoned chalice. It took a number of attempts as I stupidly hoped, like in a movie, that 40 would come bursting through the door to stop me. He was, however, uncontactable since driving off into the distance following our seaside meeting.

Upon reflection one of my biggest regrets is not continuing with the pregnancy, but I was married. Unhappily married and pregnant by another man and in the loneliest of places.

Jenny was a trooper. 'They are all a bloody waste of space', she nattered, 'Thing is Jill, we believe the lies and their spiteful stories. They are all the same. Chin up girl. You are stronger than you think.'

It wasn't long before the tablets took effect. At 11.32am I looked at what looked like a sea horse, floating in the toilet bowl. And that was it. Problem solved.

For him.

Not for me.

I would live with that decision, its associated pain, guilt and regret for the rest of my life.

And that, I figured, would be karma.

When I left the hospital David was waiting, parked outside in the car park. I felt nothing except catastrophic loss, guilt and presumed he had arrived simply to make sure I went through with the termination. I hated him for it. On reflection, I suspect he was simply trying to provide some sort of fumbled support, but he never was one for words.

In the days that followed I threw myself headlong into work and was in bed following a night shift when I heard him on the phone to 40s wife, spilling the beans. By then there was no fight left in me and I could not care less about protecting others from the truth. Their marriage was soon to head the same way as mine.

Grief is a terrible thing not only for the raw sense of loss it brings but also in how it can affect behaviour. At the time of our affair, Ian lost his dad following an illness catalysed by an accident jumping off rocks, or so I was told, on Tenby beach. Then, sometime later his younger brother was tragically killed in a road accident.

Was it these events, along with his unhappy marriage, that led him down a similar ruinous path to me, desperately searching for some happiness? Or was he simply a lying cheat who had more affairs than hot dinners and when it came to facing the music just wasn't the man he professed to be?

Who knows?

What I do know is I didn't mean to hurt anyone.

But I did. Terribly.

Things, no matter how bad, had to be faced head on, even when others were not strong enough to do so. I have lived by that mantra ever since.

I was simply chasing something in life which, at that time, I did not fully understand. It would not be until I reached fifty that I would fully comprehend why I constantly fell into this pattern of destructive behaviour. The pieces would finally make sense and complete my elusive puzzle.

Coincidentally, it was during this time that I also lost my Nan who had been the great love of my life and a stabilising force. On the day she died I kept a bedside vigil and held her hand as she took her last breath and squeezed mine in return. I went through the motions with the undertakers as the practicalities of my police training kicked in, but this was my second loss in a very short space of time. Dealing with something that you are trained for, yet means the world to you, is a whole new ball game.

Understandably and perhaps deservedly so, I had no support from David. There was by now a great chasm between us and the divorce was well under way.

I drove home late, feeling like an empty shell. I remember pulling into the side of the road on the way home as I could not see through the tears strangely settling in my eye sockets. It was as if my own eyes were willing me to drown. The night was so still, no traffic on the road anywhere and with the bright streetlamps, it was like I had driven onto a stage and someone was shining a huge spotlight on my broken heart, waiting for me to make some grand recovery.

But there wasn't one.

Gary Barlow's *Forever Love* came on the radio and with the lyrics I cried harder and more painfully than I had ever cried in my life. I had never suffered loss like this. The song still makes me cry. I then knew things had to change. I suppose you could literally call it a 'lightbulb moment'.

When I got home, David had gone to bed so there was no friendly hug or mug of tea. No condolences at all.

I slipped into the spare bedroom and contemplated Nan's passing, the final nail in the coffin of what had been a heart-breaking and near devastating run of personal loss.

Little did I know this was a feeling I needed to grow accustomed to and make my friend, as this was just the beginning. From then on life became a bit of a car crash with my personal decision-making steering me out of control.

5

Needs

I almost fell into marriage number two. He was kind to me at a time when it was me versus the world and I was extremely vulnerable. I had moved with Ella from the family home and into a grubby old police house. The carpets were so saturated with dog urine left by the previous family that you needed wellies to wade through the hallway and a gas mask to be able to breath. Woodchip wallpaper was scorched above the old economy seven electric heaters that hung off the walls, emitting so little heat they had very little purpose. It was a depressing sight, but I pulled myself together, gutted the place and transformed it into a home.

These houses were situated in a long line on a road leading into the police station.

Next door lived one of the Chief Superintendents with his wife, who it seemed struggled to cope with the expectations such a position demanded. She enjoyed the odd drink or two and rumours abounded throughout the station of regular domestic incidents between them. On one occasion an empty half vodka bottle went over the garden wall, narrowly missing an officer bringing a prisoner into custody, before smashing to smithereens on the ground. However, I don't recall either of them ever once checked into custody despite these episodes, but certain rank brings 'club' membership, a degree of privilege with the strange ability to place a magic cloak of secrecy and disappearance over anything personally inappropriate.

I never really thought of things from her point of view other than she clearly needed some support. But she was very fortunate in that she was protected from the long arm of the law.

I didn't stay there long but everyone was most kind to me, in fact some overgenerous. One of the PCs from the station came to visit and make sure I was doing okay. I remember him calling, a portly man with large feet and the bushiest beard I had ever seen. I recall always looking at it and watching intently, mesmerised to see if there were any bees, flies or small birds buzzing around within it. I was mostly disappointed, only ever noticing the odd piece of rogue ham or crumbs from his sandwiches.

He was a character and a half. Old-school upbringing and always spoke as if he was having an intelligent conversation but half the time it was utter nonsense and simply hilarious as his delivery was so serious. I recall driving back into the police station yard on one occasion when the reception door was locked, and two black people waited for assistance. Out of the blue he pulls up, winds down the window and chirps up; 'Hello our colonial cousins, how can we assist you today?'

I just wanted to curl up and hide, but he said it in such a polite and non-offensive way they simply overlooked it or maybe didn't even register it. This was a different time and political correctness was at its seedling stage. He was what he was, had his views and I doubt any amount of re-education would have changed that. And for him, why should he change? That was his upbringing, ethics and personality.

On this occasion, he called in for a supportive coffee.

'Blimey Jill, you have a lot of work ahead of you here, girl?'

He was holding a mug of coffee in his hand and I watched the steam wind its way through his beard and up towards his ears. He looked like he had smoke coming from them and it made me chuckle.

'Yes well, it's cosmetic, I will decorate and chuck some new carpet down. It will soon be a home for us.'

'Now listen.' He was now in serious tone with equally serious face on. 'There may well be times now you are single that you will have needs.'

'Needs? Tesco is only over the road I will be fine.'

'Not those sorts of needs.'

'Oh!' Here we go.

'And you will need to have someone discreet who won't make any demands on you and you can literally use just for pleasure.' I could not believe what I was hearing. How awkward.

'Jill. I am your man.'

Don't upset him, be polite. Think. Think quickly. Stop laughing.

'Okay, well thank you so much for your kind offer but I really don't think I will be interested in that for some time. And your wife? I doubt she would be so keen?'

I couldn't stop laughing as I spoke which seemed to dilute the awkwardness.

'Okay, well think about it, the offer's there.'

'Well, thank you anyway for your um, how can I put it, thoughtfulness.'

Hilarious. He hasn't even registered how inappropriate this is.

'No problem you are very welcome. What colour are you painting that wall?'

And that was it. He moved on as swiftly as that and ten minutes later was gone.

I laughed solidly for another hour or two. It was like a magic medicine.

I had first met Huw while on work experience with the police in Aberystwyth when in college and engaged to my police fiancé Nick. My first impressions should have been an accurate warning of his personality. He was a short dark-haired man, with the Rowan Atkinson look. His nickname was 'Cuddles'. He was anything but the warm image that name conveys.

I was tasked to shadow him as an observer in the traffic car and observe incidents being professionally dealt with. On a sweeping right hand bend coming down into a village was a car towing a caravan. The occupants were out of the vehicle looking a little distressed as it had clearly broken down and they were at a loss as to what to do. They saw the police car approaching and the relief on their faces was evident as they waved and smiled in our direction.

'Oh look,' Huw said, 'poor holiday makers broken down and hoping the police are going to help them.'

He started laughing to himself as we drove parallel to the caravan. 'Not today campers. Do I look like I have an AA sign on the roof?' And with that he simply raised his hand, waved back at them and accelerated away.

I was at a loss for words but found myself laughing with nervous disbelief.

Huw was stationed in Haverfordwest and had become a familiar friendly face over the years as the police family is a close one where everyone likes to know each other's business. He had his own place and after a brief courtship, we sort of fell into marriage. I don't remember any romantic proposal or unforgettable gestures, there just seemed no reason other than it simply seemed the right thing to do. He was kind and supportive of me at a very unstable time in my life. My best friend Jenny did not like him from the outset, her first recollection of him was in a pub drunk and falling over tables.

That marriage produced my second daughter, Caitlin. I planned this pregnancy; I was still desperate to fill that inner void from my termination. Huw? Well, he was a man of moods blacker than a coal man's sack. Give him a blue sky, he could definitely turn it grey. He was the opposite of David. He was a bit of a closet rebel against the establishment but in his personal world he had what I can only describe as an ominous abrasive river running through his core. He lacked the ability to follow his meanness through to the actual end and would usually become emotional and regretful once he had spoken enough words to make sure the damage was done. Everything was negative, so negative on times that it was strangely exasperatingly funny. He was similar to David in that there was never any desire to achieve new goals or partake in any opportunities that came our way. His mood was mainly black behind closed doors, but he was popular at work where he was often funny and nothing but helpful.

I was asked to travel to Cardiff to take part in a Watchdog film about utility companies taking over our home power supplies without permission. It was something exciting and a new adventure but the weather at the time was threatening snow. Huw refused to come with me on the drive to Cardiff, stating it was a load of 'bloody rubbish' and 'why would you want to do such a thing?'

Despite being fully aware I might run into tricky road conditions, he then spent the day trying to call my mobile phone constantly to see where I was, more in an interrogatory way than that of concern.

I later discovered, upon arriving home, he had insisted Ella use all her credit on her phone to call me from her mobile number to see if I gave the same explanation as to where I was. Ella was upset and this was the main root of where the rot set in with Huw.

I felt he did not embrace my first daughter Ella fully and that he treated both girls very differently. Caitlin was to sit in the front seat on the school runs, despite Ella being the eldest. Caitlin's activities were a priority over anything Ella did, and he frequently called Ella names when he thought I was out of earshot.

At one of Caitlin's early birthday parties I had ordered a big square iced birthday cake. Caitlin loved Thomas the Tank Engine and the cake sat in the middle of the party food, covered in a thick blue fondant icing. Ella loved cake and especially fondant icing.

The party was in full swing, there were a few small children, plus Huw and his parents. There was a lot of chatter and excitement as the children played, balloons floated and were chased and popped. Then came the big moment when Caitlin blew out the candles.

The cake was cut, and the children had a small slice each on matching Thomas paper plates.

I watched Ella. Every mouthful she closed her eyes with pleasure accompanied with a delicious mmm...

As she swallowed the last piece she chirped up, 'Yum, I'm having another slice,'

She jumped up from her seat whilst looking at me as if for confirmation.

I smiled and nodded my head and she headed in the direction of the table. The next thing I heard Huw mumble one cold word, just loud enough for me to hear. 'Pig.'

I looked at Huw and my eyes must have conveyed

the hatred I felt. I looked to Ella who had stopped in her tracks and dropped her head as if in shame. She had heard.

'Ellzee, come on darling, let's get that cake.'

'No, I'm okay Mummy, I'm feeling a bit sick now anyway.'

She wasn't the only one.

How dare he speak to my daughter like that, what the hell is the matter with him? Not only *my* daughter but a child. And him an adult.

Of course, I couldn't make a scene. It was Caitlin's birthday and the house was full. But later, when everyone had departed, another argument would spark.

'What the hell is your problem Huw? How dare you speak to Ella like that over a piece of bloody cake?'

'Well now, I tell you now, she is like a bloody pig, she will get fat.'

'One piece of cake? Really? And for the record, she is my daughter so you can keep your opinions to yourself.'

But the rot continued. He refused to change his ways and I watched him treat both girls very differently.

On another occasion, St David's day, both girls were dressed in the customary Welsh lady costumes. Of course, there were the usual preschool photographs which I took of them both together.

When I left the room to grab my coat, I came back to find Huw also taking photographs in front of the big bay window.

'Huw, what are you doing?' Why is Ella stood in the corner?'

'I am taking pictures of Caitlin.'

'Okay. Has Ella had a picture?'

'No, I am taking pictures of Caitlin.'

Ella looked at me, eyes wide and I ushered her over to me where she wrapped her arms around me, and we had the biggest hug.

'I know, let's go on the stairs Ellzee, there is better light and I can get some great shots.

'Caitlin, come on darling both you and your sister on the stairs.'

Photos done, I took them to school that day and upon my return he was sat in the chair in his blue checked slippers, positioned with half an eye on the TV and the other out of the window, nosing into the world outside.

I stopped by the door on my way to the kitchen. 'If you plan to do anything constructive today, perhaps learning not to be a complete prick could be top of your priorities.'

He just looked at me with his cold dark eyes and a smirk on his face.

Unbelievable.

6

Groundhog Day

We had bought a lovely new house together but there was no warmth there at all. Huw's behaviour started to make me resent him and I could feel Groundhog Day approaching in terms of where we were heading. He was my husband and we had Caitlin together. The last thing I wanted was another failed relationship. More importantly, I was wary of the effect the split would have on Caitlin. But Ella was my daughter and I was not going to stand by and watch him treat her so differently. I knew she was not happy and this worried me.

In contrast, he absolutely doted on Caitlin, in fact

too much. As she grew up and naturally tried to push the boundaries, I was the one bringing in the discipline. Huw tried to do this on many occasions, after a nudge from me, but ended up diluting the tough love into tears, crying in front of her while rambling on about, 'slippery slopes' and how if anything happened to her he would, 'surely die and not want to carry on living.'

I would often stand watching this performance with my eyes raised to heaven in despair while Caitlin, being a sharp cookie, watched nonchalantly and learned quickly how to play her hand.

I felt he bought her love as the years went on while I tried to teach her values and respect. We clashed over our parenting and especially over Ella as I stepped in to defend her.

'Why do you treat her as you do, Huw? What is your problem?'

'Well now. Caitlin is my daughter; Ella is your daughter.'

'Caitlin is *our* daughter and when we married, we came as a package and both girls should be treated the same. If you don't change your ways, we will be divorced faster than we ever took those vows. Believe me, I am not joking.'

That conversation had a consequence which illustrated how devious he was. He made little response to me, but the following day Ella returned home from school upset. She explained that when

Huw had taken her on the school run that morning, he had shouted at her;

'I tell you one thing now madam, if me and your mother split up, I will be blaming you and will come down on you like a ton of bricks.'She continued.

'I got out of the car and was crying Mum, and one of the parents asked what was wrong. He just said I had been clumsy and had jammed my hand in the car door.'

She was just seven years old and scared of him and what he might relate to me. Later, he maintained the car door story to my face.

The situation now was irreversibly beyond repair and we both agreed divorce was the best option. We did not love each other and I did not have any desire for any form of friendship with him. Ella was old enough to understand the split, especially as it made sense by the way Huw had treated her. She was unfazed. In fact, she was happy. We felt Caitlin needed no explanation as she was young and would simply adapt to spending time at both houses. I just needed a place of my own and fast.

I found a house quickly but then, having paid all my survey fees, the vendors pulled out. I was devastated but as luck would have it another came on the market on the same estate, the very same day. I viewed it at lunch time and the deal was done by teatime.

In the meantime, we had to live in separate parts of the joint house to try and alleviate the tension while the wheels of the solicitors seemed to grind forward in reverse.

I recall the climatic night he went out as both girls were away on a school trip. He liked his Guinness and, on this occasion, came home drunk. I heard the key in the door as he stumbled in, his hollow footsteps paused on the wooden flooring at the bottom of the stairs. Silence. But then my heart sank as muffled carpet footsteps slowly ascended in my direction. I prayed, wrapped in the duvet facing away from the door that he would believe I was asleep and descend just as quickly. Luck was not on my side.

A cold, grabbing hand was thrust inside the covers and I was wrenched forcefully from the sausage-like duvet surrounding me, landing on my knees so hard that the carpet stung them. He started half slurring and shouting, 'You are nothing but a fucking slag...I've heard all about you tonight and I know you are having an affair.'

Rubbing my head in bewilderment I just couldn't believe what was happening.

'How could you do this to us, and especially to Caitlin? Well now, a leopard never changes its fucking spots! I tell you now, I will be glad to be rid of you, you fucking bitch!'

At this point I was completely disorientated; he was

accusing me of an affair when I had been nothing but faithful and seemed to be strangely justifying himself and his actions. I was struggling, at this juncture, to understand why.

Things were getting out of hand, so I managed to get to my feet and push past him as he stumbled backward into the bedroom wall. I somehow got myself down the narrow staircase, all the time hearing him close behind as he slid down a few steps and lost his footing. My plan was to get my coat even though I was in pyjamas and just get the hell out of there.

'Calm down Huw, you are drunk...I'm going to leave so just go to bed.'

'You aren't going anywhere darlin', cos I'm going to smash that fucking Audi TT of yours to bits, every panel I will smash with a fucking rolling pin!'

My car was parked on the drive and I knew I had to get the keys. There was no question he was going to do it as I could hear him rummaging in the kitchen drawer before he reappeared in the lounge doorway, arms aloft in triumphant stance shaking the rolling pin like some sort of angry orchestral conductor.

At the same time, I found the keys.

'Yes, that's right, take your keys. By the time I finish the only place you will be driving to is the fucking scrapyard.'

He was now blocking the door.

'Please Huw, this is stupid, just let me pass. I

promise I will leave here, and you can go to bed. I won't say a word about this to anyone.'

'I don't give a fuck who you tell, but you love that car so I'm going to smash what you love to pieces,' and he spun around, heading for the front door.

In sheer panic I launched myself toward him and the door hoping the force of my body would knock him sideways just enough for me to escape, get in the car and drive away.

Unfortunately, he remained solid and I bounced off him backwards and came crashing to the floor, striking the side of my head on the corner of the marble fireplace as I did so. The pain felt like an ice pick to my temple and I remember feeling the tears starting to stream down my face as I scrambled to my feet to find him slouched against the chair, sobbing.

'What have I done? I'm going to call the police and hand myself in and tell them I have beaten my wife.'

He picked up the phone and started dialling 999.

'Hello,' he slurred, 'Police emergency...PC Evans 659 Haverfordwest, I have assaulted my wife. Best you come here pronto.'

I grabbed the phone, but he pushed me off 'Fuck off me, you bitch.'

I tried in vain to stop this course of destruction he was on, but it was no good. He managed to place the call, fully identified himself, complete with our address.

The blue lights were soon flashing in the driveway.

I denied any assault, albeit technically I could have pushed it, but essentially, I had launched my body at him in the doorway and the rebound was the result. My priority was protecting Caitlin and whatever the situation between us was, there was no way I could see Huw be investigated and under pressure with his job.

I left willingly that night and went to Jenny's house. When we returned the next morning all my clothes had been removed from the house and placed in the middle of the lawn where they formed a giant heap of smouldering bonfire. We just stood there in silence and disbelief, watching the smoke rise in front of our tired eyes, before Jenny piped up 'Well you won't be able to wear those again.'

I just turned to look at her kind face as the tears resumed.

It later emerged it was he who had apparently been unfaithful and thus the drink-fuelled episode had been a classic display of justifying his own guilt, not mine.

We managed to agree that I would simply take enough equity from the house to enable me to put a deposit down on my new place. I did not push for half shares as basically he had owned a house before I came along, and I felt it only right that he had back fully what he put into our home. Nevertheless, it didn't stop him putting the word around the station that I had taken him to the cleaners for every penny and even stripped the lightbulbs and curtains from under his feet.

My dabble into police officers had been less than successful.

In time and upon later reflection I felt a little like Goldilocks and the porridge. David was too weak, Huw was far too bitter and the third, 40, well, just right but seemingly only through my distorted vision. It's hard to keep optimistic when bitten so many times but to give up all hope means you lose positivity in life. It is true that when one door closes it does so for a reason, I just didn't expect another, equally as bad, to open. I was kind of scared to open any more, except my own front door and that, for a time, was exactly what I did.

I think there is a statistic that says that most people who are single are only single by choice. Although battered and bruised, I spent the next year or two firmly unattached and focused on the children and my career.

7

Home Sweet Home

On the day I was handed the keys to our new home I felt like I had just been released from prison. It had been a hard time for us both, but we managed to keep things relatively amicable, partly I suspect due to the fact that I was agreeing to leave with far less financially than I was entitled to and in return the girls remained living with me. Ella of course was delighted and relieved but as for Caitlin, she was being taken from living with a dad who doted on her and could seemingly do no wrong.

I spent my last night at the old house in a lukewarm bath, shivering and staring at the goose bumps on my legs. The house was cold, it had not really been lived in as Huw had kept a low profile while I prepared to move out. It felt like a lifeless soul, its heart ripped mercilessly from within. I was glad to be shutting that door for the final time, but knowing Huw had to remain in such an unpleasant environment made me sad and I still felt sorry for him.

Damn! I always felt sorry for them.

The slow drip of the tap empathised with me as I sat there, head on knees, sobbing that life had once again come to this.

I vowed that night to use those feelings to cement my next path of solely focusing on my children and my career. One positive in this tumultuous period had been passing my Sergeant's exam on the first attempt and shortly afterwards being promoted to shift sergeant in Haverfordwest.

This will be a new start, I told myself.

The next morning, slowly turning the key in my new front door I stepped inside and felt the warmth envelop me as I closed my eyes and took a deep breath. I felt safe, it felt right.

The girls loved the excitement of it all. It was three-bedroom house so they both had their own room upstairs, next to my double bedroom and the bathroom.

Downstairs there was a kitchen, cloakroom and large spacious lounge. The neighbours were lovely, and the kids would be able to safely walk to school and back as they grew up, without issue.

I redecorated and ordered new furniture to replace what I had left behind.

The new house soon became a home and things started to settle down…for a while.

I decided to buy the girls a rabbit. He was a grey, lop-eared rabbit with the cutest furry face but I think he was deaf as he had this strange habit of rocking his head back and forth in a trance like state. I bought a large rabbit hutch and run and Bertie the rabbit became the only new male addition to our home.

One evening my phone went off.

Text message. *Enjoying your cosy night in, are you?*

It was Huw.

I ignored it. He was clearly looking for a reaction

Beep Beep. A second message: *Rabbit looks good in his hutch.*

I hadn't told Huw about the rabbit but there was every chance Caitlin had.

I was feeling a little uneasy now as the next message soon followed. *I'm outside, in the garden behind the hutch, I can see you through the patio doors.*

'Mummy, who's texting?' Ella had leaned over and read the message over my shoulder.

'Who is it Mummy, who is outside?'

'Shhtt, keep your voice down darling. Don't worry, it's only Huw. I will sort this now.'

But I felt uneasy. *Fatal Attraction* was a movie I had

watched, and I was more concerned as to whether Bertie was still in his hutch, alive and kicking. I went to the kitchen to check he was not boiling in a pot on the hob and panic over, I peered out through the patio doors into the darkness of the garden. I heard Ella thundering up the stairs and the next thing, the jingling of the wooden curtain rings as they were thrust open, followed by the rattling of a window latch opening above me. I saw a flashlight erratically scanning the garden. The red of Bertie's eyes flashed in front of me as they caught the light. Then her voice.

'If you have hurt my rabbit, I swear I will throw a brick down at you! Come out and show yourself, you coward!'

Ella. She had at last found her voice and she was not afraid to use it.

She kept the flashlight on while I ventured out into the cold.

'Mum, check for any footprints in the grass around Bertie.'

My heart was beating fast, but I laughed to myself. My girl was a budding detective.

But there was nothing. He was not in the garden at all. It was just another form of mind game, something Huw seemed to relish.

It took a long time to stop.

Kevin and Hannah were friends of mine. We had become close as Kevin was also a sergeant at

Haverfordwest and together we supervised the same shift, known as Code 3. He was the custody sergeant while I covered the street or everything outside of custody.

We decided to have a night out and my girls slept over at theirs. Our evening was cut short as we received a frantic phone call from the babysitter. We were leaving a pub in a street where phone signal was either non-existent or intermittent. I could see Hannah waving her phone around to try and grab signal whilst simultaneously shouting, 'What? What has he done?'

I instinctively knew something was wrong.

'Jill, taxi now! Kevin shouted, Huw is at the house kicking off.'

My heart sank as we piled into a nearby cab and gave instructions to the driver, like we were in some sort of action film.

'Prendergast', shouted Kevin. 'As fast as you can.'

We arrived at the house and all was quiet outside but inside was a different story. The sitter was in a terrible state, stating Huw had turned up, banging the door like a banshee and demanding that Caitlin, asleep in bed, leave with him. The sitter had opened the door where she saw him leaned against the porch, slurring his words and then using his foot as a doorstop when she tried to close it. She only managed to secure it closed by ramming it on to his foot so that when he pulled it away in pain, she could lock it.

As she loudly carried out her threat to call Hannah and Kevin on the phone, he had unsurprisingly made a sharp exit.

The following morning the police Inspector, a fan of Huw's, visited to 'smooth things over' and ensure the matter was firmly swept under the carpet with no complaint forthcoming.

Part of me was furious, as was Hannah, but the other part was relieved he had got off the hook. Again, for Caitlin's sake.

I was in a catch 22. I believed he should be punished for his behaviour but did not want Caitlin hurt in the process. He was, after all, her dad.

The climax came when he sent me a single text message shortly after this incident. It came on its own and was unrelated to any conversation by text or otherwise. Simple and short. *Tell Caitlin I love her*

It was sent with what I felt was a suicidal connotation as he was quite capable of telling her this himself when he saw her daily so I knew what he was suggesting. Without hesitation, I called it in to the police station. Whether it was the embarrassment of that police visit that brought him to his senses, I am not altogether sure. What I do know is when he gave up his destructive behaviour it was a huge relief for us all.

Huw should have been disciplined for his actions, but it was the same old story prevalent throughout

Dyfed Powys Police and, I expect, many other forces and organisations. One rule and standard does not apply to all, it is more a case of whether your face fits and if you have a good sponsor to cover your back. If you do, you can seemingly break the law, act inappropriately and still escape punishment.

His behaviour was minor compared to others.

One troubled officer with ambition to climb the ranks went for a night out in Llanelli and was caught urinating in a public place for which he received a fixed penalty fine following arrest. The custody unit did not identify that he was a serving officer within the Force as he was not from that division and he failed to mention it.

Police officers are not supposed to be involved in any form of criminality no matter how minor. If that happens the Professional Standards department or as I used to call them 'shiny shoe brigade' got involved and such behaviour would undoubtedly result in an internal investigation often culminating in a hearing. The hearing would consist of a panel of senior police officers, a little bit like a court of law except that the burden of proof was far less. The panel does not have to prove the case against you beyond all reasonable doubt but simply on a balance of probabilities. The sanctions? These ranged from a warning to dismissal but in his case, the police officer paid the fine, swerved all disciplinary investigations and the matter mysteriously disappeared.

A few months later he was the talk of the station as the rumours circulated that he was part of a group of officers who attended a joint birthday party for two members of police staff. A coach was booked to return them home. He proceeded to stagger up and down the aisle, allegedly exposing himself and simultaneously distracting the bus driver who desperately tried to drive and control the situation. This officer's grand finale was to produce a fountain of golden urine which ran like a river down the centre of the bus. He paid harshly for his act of public order in that he received no sanction at all. Nothing. Instead he climbed the ranks to Divisional Commander.

I bonded with my team fantastically well. Sergeant Kevin Jones was renowned for being one of the loudest and most direct characters on the division. He was practical, down to earth and through him I learned how to get that same balance. Kevin was always laughing and loved his food, he was like the cookie monster but with stripes on his shoulder; nothing was safe.

Kevin later recounted to me how many people, especially some policewomen, sympathised with him prior to my arrival, stating he would need luck as I was 'bloody hard work'. Kevin was wise enough to always know there are two sides to a story and he held his judgement. We hit it off from day one and hence I was introduced to his partner, Hannah, who became a good friend.

The general public perception of the police service is that it is one family, closing ranks in times of adversity and equally supporting one another to provide an efficient, reliable service. That is not the reality. There are a lot of jealous people circulating in each rank and those that are hungry for promotion will not think twice about choosing to keep quiet over matters that may affect their prospects, as opposed to doing the right thing by others. The pettiness of some of the senior ranks toward those below is laughable, often wasting time turning minor issues into mountains for the sake of flexing their power.

During one night shift I had concerns over my car which had been damaged while left in the public car park at the station. I parked it in the rear yard, which was more secure and where the patrol and police vehicles were kept.

The duty inspector resembled a child in both appearance and mannerism. He was short with a boyish face and I had known him for some time as he was a detective constable before his attempt to ascend the ranks. He walked everywhere in a kind of panic, like a child who had momentarily but simultaneously lost his mother and comfort blanket.

He was eager to make an impression and reach dizzier heights as quickly as his fervent legs would take him there.

Having just finished the night shift briefing with my team I received a phone call from him.

'Sergeant Evans, please can you remove your personal vehicle from the rear yard, it is for police vehicles only.'

Hmm. 'Sir, my vehicle has already been damaged and as the rear yard is quiet on nights, I feel it's doing no harm to anyone and is safer there.'

There was, incidentally, no official restriction on vehicles entering this area.

'Sergeant, that yard is for police vehicles only.'

'Sir, it is my vehicle, the same as yours is parked there, and I am not prepared to move it.'

'Sergeant, if you don't move it, I will place you on a charge for disobeying an order.'

'Sir, I am declining for good reason, it is not effecting anyone, and it's just a parked car!'

'So, you are refusing?'

'Sir, I am declining. Yes.'

'Very well.'

I simply thought he was having a tantrum as clearly something had upset him, and this seemed such a petty matter to get upset about.

I believed that was the end of it until the next day when I was duly summonsed to his office where he demanded my pocket notebook and scrawled an official entry about my 'disobedience.' He puffed his chest out and pulled his shoulders back as he handed the weathered notebook back to me and I felt like I should congratulate him, like a mother congratulating her son on being presented with his first nursery painting.

I resisted the urge, thanked him and fortunately managed to still sleep soundly that night.

Incidents that merited action were often overlooked to focus on the trivial which summed up the mentality of many in rank. It was far easier to pull rank in petty situations to try and demonstrate they had this skill but to pursue this course of action against those 'in the gentleman's club' or put simply pulling rank against those who were 'in favour' was a far more risky business. The ladder to promotion would then become a lot greasier and this was not a gamble that many were willing to take.

My reputation for being a little outspoken suddenly went before me. I was portrayed by some as awkward when I simply thought logically. I combined this with an element of common sense when resolving problems while keeping things practical and real. I appropriately challenged things that did not make sense to me but often this was labelled as confrontation.

I wasn't afraid to make decisions but prior to doing so, I would always consult my team, because as the sergeant the buck stopped with me. I was acutely aware they all had different skills, abilities and experiences, which when put together would solve any issue. That gave every member validity in my eyes and made work something to enjoy and look forward to. Happy staff were always productive ones.

I was quite a strong woman who could deal with anything the public or colleagues tried to throw at me. I prided myself on being professional and yes, I did set high standards. An inspector who I later encountered as my welfare officer, Inspector Hayes, once said that my standards were too high and that I should lower them. I was astounded and always maintained the ethos that I was paid to do a job well and expected the same dedication from my team. As a result, those that did not warm to me were often lazy and incompetent, as I would challenge them and have the same expectation of them as of everyone else I supervised, whatever their gender.

8

Calamity Jane

There had been a report of a person who had been seen waving a gun about in a residential area.

My team was on shift and following an impromptu briefing and having been given the description of the male, we were able to make a pretty good guess using our local knowledge of who the individual responsible was likely to be.

The mention of guns alerted what was then called the ARV (armed response vehicle) and they were summoned from the force area to descend in Haverfordwest for a tactical briefing by the chief inspector. This would be where decisions would be made regarding how to approach the situation and ultimately detain the alleged offender safely and without harm to the public.

I attended the briefing. There were approximately sixty officers there, armed and ready to be deployed.

'Sir,' I said, 'we believe this individual to be a local character judging by the description, his behaviour and the particular area he was seen in.'

I knew this individual, a troubled lad but more of an attention seeker with learning disabilities, as opposed a dangerous gunman on the loose. I had also dealt with him several times and so he knew me, and we had a rapport.

The chief inspector replied, 'Sergeant, we cannot be sure of that so leave this operation to the response units. You and your team can be released.'

I raised my eyes and sighed. Well, how nice. Thank you very much!

He cleared his throat, 'So as I was saying, before being interrupted, we will deploy to the local church hall in the area he was last seen in where there will be a further tactical briefing.'

More talk, less decision-making and our input dismissed. My team regrouped. Heads down.

'Okay, fuck it, let's go pay the mother a visit. Just because we are dismissed from their operation doesn't stop us having our own.'

Their faces perked up and we were off, our little panda cars sped out of the yard leaving the Range

Rovers idling, still ruminating about their next move.

We arrived at the mothers' house.

'Hi, I am so sorry to bother you, but we have a little mystery we need to solve.'

'Of course, Jill, no problem. Come in. What has he done now?'

'Okay well, it's nothing to worry about but we have had a report of a male person matching your son's description waving a gun around outside.'

She raised her eyes in exasperation. 'Hang on a sec.'

She left the room and re-entered moments later with a black plastic water pistol.

'I told the silly bastard that someone around here would report him, but he insisted on messing about and trying to squirt people.'

We all breathed a sigh of relief.

'Ah, I thought as much,' I said, 'Where is he now?'

'Your guess is as good as mine love, but when I get my hands on the little shit, water pistols will be the least of his worries.'

'Ok, alright if I take this?' I reached for the water pistol.

She nodded.

'Do me a favour and give us a shout when he appears, and we will come have a little chat. I will go and call off the cavalry.'

And with that we were out the door, like the Scooby Doo gang, meddling kids jubilant that we, the local team, had solved the mystery.

I radioed back in to update Kevin.

'He-he,' he mumbled through a mouthful of food, 'that'll teach 'em not to listen.'

'Kev, what are you eating?'

'I dunno, someone left their sandwich box in custody, I think it's a chicken sandwich?'

I laughed

'Right look, I'm going to go the church hall now to call off the guns, he is hiding out somewhere, so once he resurfaces his mam will bell us.'

'Okay. Hurry back and bring back some biscuits with you, family pack and preferably custard creamy ones, I'm bloody starving.'

I was still laughing as I walked into the hall, which was choc full, unlike Kevin's stomach.

The superintendent in charge of the operation was old-school. A short, stout man with a strong Welsh accent. I liked him, he was straight, and you knew exactly where you stood. He would bollock you as opposed to pull rank through the disciplinary channel and he would deal with you directly, not cloak and dagger. I liked that and respected him for it.

The briefing was full flow.

'So, this individual was last seen at the bottom of Court Road, so I suggest we -'

'Sir, can I have a word?'

Heads slowly spun around, and he raised his eyes.

'Sergeant Evans, what now? We are in the middle

of a briefing, whatever you have got to say can wait till the end.'

'Oh, okay,' I replied and, as I stood at the back of the room, I casually put my forefinger through the trigger guard of the plastic gun and raised my hand to shoulder height while spinning the gun around on my finger, Calamity Jayne style. Nobody took the slightest bit of notice of what I was doing and the whole briefing went on at least another half hour before deployment.

'Right, Jill bach (Welsh word for 'little', often added on to a name or word by Welsh speakers, signifying warmth or familiarity), what on earth is so important?'

As he spoke his eyes shifted sideways to my elevated hand, saw the gun and suddenly widened as if popping out of his head on slinky springs.

'It was as we thought, sir, and the gun was a water pistol, in fact this very one.'

'What? How did you get hold of it?'

'I called at his house and his mother gave it to me.'

'Bloody hell woman…all units stand down.'

'Evans, I will see you in half an hour back in my office.'

And so, the day ended with the wrath of his tongue, for not following tactical procedure and potentially putting my life in danger. But there was no pocketbook entry.

'Evans, you are dismissed. Get out of my bloody

sight.'

'Okay boss.'

I turned and walked towards the door

'Sergeant Evans? One last thing before you go.'

'Yes, sir?'

'Bloody good work from you and your team.'

I smiled as I climbed the stairs back to the coalface.

9

The Cauldron

Female recruits were on the increase. There was a tightly knit click of female officers at the station who would get together, whispering about men, general gossip and the next night out. I was never included in that group and had no desire to be part of it. I kept my own council and as a result they considered me aloof.

I think they had an issue with my supervisory role, more so that I had a good professional relationship with most of the male officers who found me to be a half decent sergeant. Also, I kept myself fit, I was slim and was reasonably popular with the guys I supervised, and this group of women were fickle things. There was a lot of insecurity and jealousy floating about. I may have bent the rules just enough to incorporate common sense, but I never broke the rules and I certainly had the utmost respect and passion for the role I performed.

One of the main characters in this group was a WPC who was hungry for any gossip circulating the station corridors. She was a competent police officer when she put her mind to it but had an openly dramatic love life which tended to sway the general opinion that she was mainly a drama queen and thus not taken seriously. She enjoyed a social drink and at the wedding of a fellow officer, she perceived what she felt was her boyfriend becoming a little too friendly with another member of the 'click' and, as a result, momentarily turned a happy occasion into an alcohol-fuelled physical showdown.

However, as was form, she was another who avoided sanction and shortly afterwards was back arresting people for the very behaviour she had a penchant for displaying herself.

Two female probationers were assigned to the station.

The first was older and struggled with her fitness, which demonstrated the slow decline in the standard of recruit. She had come from an office job as a school secretary and the jump was vast.

One bright but cold Sunday morning the first job for all, including me, was to wash the police vehicles and check the oil and water. This was a regular Sunday morning ritual and I always chose to do this with my team as I led by example.

'Okay you lot, let's get these cars out of the way.'

As the group put their mugs back on the tray this WPC piped up, 'What would you like me to do?'

'Down the wash now, the cars have to be cleaned.'

'It's okay, I don't do cars.'

'Well, I'm afraid you do now, down the wash please.'

Her face was like thunder.

Within days the superintendent summoned me to his office to be told I was being investigated for bullying, following a complaint received from her. In addition, a second complaint made by another female probationer had been added in the mix.

I had completed a constructive staff appraisal for the latter where we concluded that there were areas of the role she was struggling with and needed improvement. She, like her colleague, was struggling to make decisions and to progress, despite a lot of help channelled her way. Officers were complaining about having to carry her and I openly highlighted and discussed these issues with her. An agreed plan of action was put in place. Shortly afterwards I found her crying in the ladies' toilet.

'I just wish I could be more like you.'

I explained kindly that experience did not come overnight, gave her an encouraging hug and urged her to keep positive.

These two, however, were accepted members of the 'click' and so it was no surprise that both attempted to bring me down for simply treating them equally and having the same expectation of them as I did the rest of the team.

But it didn't matter, officially I was now under investigation for bullying by the force's Professional Standards department. The investigation lasted three months and concluded with a decision to provide me with 'words of advice'. This is the outcome where a complaint is made against an officer, but insufficient evidence is found to bring internal charges against them. But rather than say there is no case to answer, the police's Professional Standards department must always leave those unfavoured with some little marked card and in my case, it was those meaningless three little words.

Three months of hassle for simply doing my job.

One has now left the job with stress, spending much of her time prior to that on paid sick leave. The second, I'm reliably informed, has somehow made it to a poorly rated sergeant.

So, life at work was far from boring and, aside from these minor interferences, I was doing well, happy in my world and for once glad to be free of personal torment. Work issues were just that – work issues - and I threw myself headlong into it with relish. But as time went on, I began to feel lonely. Once the children had gone to bed there was nobody to sit and discuss the day with and I began to wonder whether I should listen to my friends and dip my toe back in the water.

10

The Guvnor

Like everything in life, internet dating has its pros and cons. I quickly worked out that it had three distinct stages to pass before there was any realistic prospect of success. After the initial physical attraction, the first stage is the textual chemistry.

It is so easy to hide behind a keyboard but at the same time this is an important stage as it's where you get an initial feeling about the person you are corresponding with, without having met. It is also the stage where many fall in love with the words or image they conceive of that person, often far from the actual reality but something your mind wishes, wants or hopes. It's actually quite a vulnerable time on the keyboard and it isn't a failsafe from weirdos. I recall reading a guy's profile where he narrated that he had no intention of bringing up anyone else's kids or being a bank for his potential new girlfriend. Of course, I had to engage him in conversation, purely because of his unfortunate attitude. I had never looked to a partner to provide for me or mine that was my job, so his profile irritated me from the outset.

His picture displayed him standing proudly in what seemed to be his large, lavish living room. Unfortunately, he had failed to move an old style upright hoover with a large grey tatty dust bag attached. It was just out of the shot. I found myself asking him whether that was a recent picture of him with his last girlfriend and, as predicted, it did the trick. The reply was a tirade of abuse about women in general and clearly outed him for the person he was.

This first texting stage with Dean was back and forth like an M134 minigun, a 7.62mm calibre gun fired at a superfast pace of 6000 rounds per minute. We had instant rapport and at times it was like a championship tennis match, each of us wanting to win the game, set, in fact the whole damn match in terms of the speed of the replies and witty repartee. They were general fact-finding messages and I was relieved that he didn't make the schoolboy error of trying to manipulate the conversation around to sex with the casual inclusion of erect body part pictures. This, quite frankly, would have put a swift emergency stop on the conversation. Apparently, it is common in these exchanges.

We progressed to stage two fairly swiftly, a reflection of my character, being direct with little fuss or any time for game playing. This was where I had to hear his voice for the first time and decide whether the image I had built so far, matched the reality.

I knew he was a Londoner so expected a typical South East London accent and I was pretty accurate in my prediction. My phone rang at precisely the time we agreed.

'Hello darlin'... how are you?'

His voice was deep and so relaxed he could have been horizontal and had a smoothness like a marshmallow being slowly enveloped in a cascade of silky melted chocolate. Its sound filled me with a mixture of excitement and relief that the illusion was not shattered.

Keep calm, I said to myself, it's the new superpower. Don't be too keen.

'Hey, I'm all good here, just caught your call.'

With that he burst out laughing.

'You sound nothing like Vanessa from Gavin and Stacey.'

'Ha-ha, well no, London boy, I am not from Barry. You see, we don't all speak the same in Wales, you know boyo.'

And from there the laughter and conversation flowed, about nothing in particular, but sufficient to know he didn't sound like a complete dead loss and was definitely worth spending some of my free mobile call allowance on. More importantly, the laughter and light-hearted conversation was like an almighty breath of fresh air with the added safety that I was able to control it from a distance and keep things at my pace.

I learned that he was a businessman based in central London, running his own distribution company supplying some big High Street retailers. He was separated from his wife with whom he had two daughters and was in the process of divorce. That did not concern me, as at thirty-years old and with similar history, I figured anyone I potentially met would have baggage. It would somehow be more cause for concern if they didn't.

'I have my own male toiletries range.'

Oh no, here comes the bullshit, I thought. 'Yer… right, I'm sure you do.'

'No, I do! Tell you what, take a trip to your nearest Superdrug store, you do have them in Wales, yes? Look in the men's toiletries section for The Guvnor range.'

'Yeh, yeh, it's fine Dean, you don't need to overcook trying to impress me.'

'Really darlin',' his voice drawled, 'Just go look.'

Was he serious? 'Okay, well you know I may just do that when I've time.' Ice cold response.

As soon as the call ended, I hot footed it down to Superdrug and there, on the shelf, was 'The Guvnor Range'.

It was a selection of three items' a men's body wash called 'Beat the Filth', a moisturiser labelled 'Protection' and finally an extra strong hair gel called 'It's a Stick Up'.

I picked up a tube and looked on the back and there was his picture right before my eyes. I couldn't believe it, he wasn't joking at all.

I found myself muttering, 'Bloody hell' aloud, oblivious to those around me, as I flipped the tube around from front to back in my clammy hand. Never had a simple tube of shower gel had such a profound effect on me.

I returned home and logged on to the internet where my naturally questioning nature told me I needed to look a bit more deeply into this, I googled 'The Guvnor Range'. At this stage I only had a brief insight into Dean through texts and phone calls and so I was excited to find out as much as I could about him, as would anyone in my position. It was simple human nature. Up popped the website advertising the same products I had seen in the store along with the history of the business, its founders (Dean being one), and endorsements from celebrities; Vinnie Jones, Ray Winston and Guy Richie to name but a few.

Dean was pictured dressed in a T-shirt and jeans leaning up against the bonnet of a silver Jaguar XK8 convertible, displaying a private plate, 'D7 GUV'. This was the first full size picture I had seen of him and he looked exactly as I had imagined; stocky, chunky and quite simply someone who could handle themselves. All the things I suppose that many women would look for in a man. There was also a write-up which gave a little personal insight into him:

At 37, Dean is a married man with two beautiful girls and his own booming business. Dean started out as a carpenter and moved on to a job in a warehouse where he was working for a mogul who made him a warehouse manager. He proved himself to be a big player and they became distribution partners. Already a part owner in Mr Mascara and in a distribution partnership for Tweezer man, Guam and Eco tan, it was only a matter of time before he came up with a range of his own.

My mouth fell open in amazement as I read it. He had told me he was in distribution, but he hadn't mentioned any big names and to be fair, the list was quite impressive. The fact that he hadn't name dropped gave him a few extra brownie points.

I quickly did the maths by checking the copyright on the article, which was dated 2004. Two years ago, so entirely feasible that he was separated and going through the process of divorce. Add the fact that I already knew about his daughters and now there was this cool for cats website with his products as he'd described, there was nothing that rang any warning bells for me. In fact, I simply couldn't believe my luck.

I read the write-up for the products, all of which had connotations with prison and robberies

It's a Stick Up...look at the price tag, you won't even have to rob a bank to afford a tube.

Beat the Filth...this gentle, effective and revitalising body and hair wash will soon have you cleaner than your average criminal record.

I laughed at the descriptions, firstly as the marketing tactics were so smart using words to make an instant connection with customers aimed cleverly to drive the sales, and secondly as they described in a bold and flippant way the world that I fought and worked so hard to contain. I had yet to mention my occupation to Dean but now it became even more strangely ironic, if not amusing.

Later that day we spoke, his London drawl so calm and assured.

'My darling, one thing you will learn about me is that I will never lie to you. Great marketing isn't it? What was it you said you did for a living again?'

I laughed and thought, 'don't mention police sergeant yet. He will likely run a mile, most men do and things are going so well'. 'Well, nothing as amazing as you, I just work in the legal industry, pretty boring stuff in comparison.'

'Oh, that's pretty cool, brains as well as beauty.'

And so, the conversation flowed.

During the day we would text countless times and talk maybe once or twice. There was never a time that I could not reach him on his mobile and he gave me his office number as a backup in case I should ever need it. In fact, I rang this number numerous times from different phones and on each occasion the receptionist answered with the company greeting and put me through to him without hesitation.

It wasn't long before we decided to set a date to meet, stage three of my internet dating plan.

Cardiff was the midway point for both of us so it was agreed he would stay overnight in a hotel so we could have dinner and relax. My brother had an apartment in Cardiff Bay at the time and on a weekend when my girls had each gone to stay with their respective dads, I arranged to stay at his place.

Dean booked into the Ibis Hotel and we arranged for a 3pm meeting in the bar. As I walked toward the building my heart was thumping in my chest. I was so damn nervous, more so I think as things had been going so well and I knew that if that mutual instant physical attraction wasn't there when we met, the happiest of few weeks would soon be coming to an end.

I pushed the glass door and walked cautiously across the tiled floor. The click of my heels seemed to fill the half empty bar as customers chatted and people watched from their seats and naturally turned their heads upon hearing me enter.

Oh, God where is he, will I even recognise him in real life?

A stocky figure slowly turned on his revolving stool at the bar and his eyes met mine. His pupils swelled like ink dropped from a pipette on to blotting paper. 'Jill, gin and tonic on the rocks?'

I recognised the smooth low voice and the eyes straight away.

'Uhm, yes, fabulous thank you,' I stammered, trying hard to maintain an air of confidence.

'Let me take your coat, you look amazing. Shall we take these over to somewhere quieter?'

'He's is so bloody cool, pull yourself together', I thought.

He nodded towards the window booth. It was a cold, grey day in Cardiff but there was a cosy and a relaxed atmosphere in the bar, the lighting giving it a warm ambience as it reflected off the rich, oxblood red leather seating.

I, on the other hand, was in a battle with myself, trying to remain outwardly confident while controlling the nerves that were ripping my insides apart. He looked exactly as I imagined and was the perfect gentleman, which was a blinding result but simply made me even more hopeful for things to go well.

'So, Dean, how was your trip down?'

'It was great, I've parked just outside. That's my car under the bridge.'

As he pointed, I glanced across, glass in hand, and spotted a new silver BMW 3 series convertible with a black hood. I smiled: Typical, he would have to have the car that I have always wanted to own.

'What's that noise?' I said, looking around bewildered as I could hear a jingling noise coming from somewhere. I was so caught up in the moment that I failed to realise where it was coming from.

'It's the ice in your glass Jill, you are shaking,' he said as he leaned back in his seat.

I looked at my hand as if for confirmation and then raised my eyes to his.

Our laughter was loud and simultaneous, but I was forever thankful to those few cubes in my glass as they literally did break the ice that day.

We had dinner that night at a curry house of my choosing and in true gentlemanly fashion, he made sure I was comfortably seated before taking his place in the seat opposite me. As he took his first mouthful of chicken curry I chose to get the career clarification over with. My decision was conveniently helped by the appearance of a well-behaved stag party, the stag locked into a pair of handcuffs.

'Blimey,' Dean said, 'I remember them old days, poor bugger, he wouldn't look so happy if he knew what I did about marriage.'

I laughed in agreement

'Mind you, those pink handcuffs look tasty, I bet you've never owned a pair of them?' He chuckled as he put the fork to his mouth and took a mouthful of food.

'Hmm, not in pink, no, but I have a nice black rigid pair.'

He looked up and his eyes widened with a cheeky glint. 'I didn't put you down as the handcuff type.'

I laughed. 'I bet you didn't put me down for the uniform type either, but they kind of come with the territory.'

He stopped chewing now and looked straight at me

'What do you mean? Solicitors don't wear uniforms?'

'I know,' I replied, 'but police sergeants do.'

The curry must have caught his throat because something made him start coughing with such force that his eyes started to stream, and he grabbed the glass of water in front of him and gulped it down in one.

'Dean, are you ok? I haven't mentioned it before as it's kind of off-putting to many guys and it's just that things have been going so well and...'

He cut me off

'No, no, it's fine,' he spluttered, 'The Old Bill are the pillar of society darlin', that doesn't cause me any issues at all.'

He kept laughing about this revelation for the rest

of the night, passing it off as it being the last thing he would expect me to do. I wasn't aware at that stage how big this revelation must have been to him; I was simply relieved it was out there and he was cool with it.

Later that evening he escorted me safely into my taxi home. I really wasn't used to being treated so well and the fact that he was so mature in both demeanour and conversation was a refreshing change.

The next morning, I walked over to the hotel and we had breakfast before it was time for the goodbyes. I always hated goodbyes, and this became a joke between us as the relationship progressed, but this first one felt unusually difficult, like I had known him forever. Within minutes of him driving away my phone was ringing and we chatted for most of his journey back to London.

I learned a lot of things about him at that first meeting.

Following his separation, he had a 'bachelor pad' where, for some time, he led a bachelor lifestyle with the ladies. But he was looking for more stability. It was for that reason he said he would never want me to stay at his place as the neighbours would think I was just another 'bird' when for him, this wasn't the case at all. I found this perfectly feasible at the time, especially as he gave me his actual home address should I ever need it and, in any case, I was not that concerned. Due to the distance we had agreed to meet up only every other weekend which would work out perfectly with both our respective children. My girls stayed with their dads on the same weekend and he said he would rearrange his access to match. For a while, we could keep our worlds conveniently apart until the time was right to merge them.

The last thing I wanted was to rush into the ins and outs of his living arrangements.

Within weeks my thirty-eighth birthday arrived, and Dean surprised me with a weekend away. I met him at the hotel and was booked into a suite with flowers, champagne... and a tastefully chosen pair of knee length all leather boots. They would not have been something I would have bought myself as, at that time, I could only dream of having nice things and could not justify that sort of expense. But it was more than that.

The thought he had put into the gift made me feel like I had actually celebrated a birthday as opposed to birthdays in the past where I had received a television, a toaster or something else needed for the house to simply and conveniently 'kill two birds with one stone'.

I wasn't used to being treated like this, my feelings and happiness had suddenly become a priority on those weekends and my faith in love was starting to slowly regenerate.

Maybe all the heartache of the past had meant that I deserved happiness and to be treated well. I told myself to relax and give this a chance.

My thoughts became less cynical and positivity began to cautiously re-emerge.

The pattern of meeting every other weekend, work shifts permitting, continued. For the main I travelled to London, mostly my choice as I wasn't ready to introduce anyone new to the children. The weekends away were always exciting so I really didn't mind.

I was very quickly introduced to his mum and her partner and then his sisters, Nan, nephews and nieces. I went to their homes and I visited his place of work where I met the workforce and the PA whom I had often spoken to on the phone. I saw the warehouse. I saw the products in the warehouse. I drove his vehicles and was introduced to his friends. In summary I was integrated publicly and proudly into his personal space.

One weekend, 'The Guvnor Range' was sponsoring a race meeting at Brands Hatch. I travelled up for the weekend and stayed with Dean's mum. We had hit it off straight away and she was clearly hugely supportive of Dean and his business. She would often talk openly of his marriage that had failed and how upset she was that his two girls had become estranged and she did not see them. I did not ask any questions about the ex-wife but gained the impression she was considered high maintenance, no doubt as most ex-wives are probably branded. I am unsure whether I came to this conclusion due to the fact that her description was the complete opposite to me or whether I was simply used to my view of the world where I worked hard for what we had and did not expect to be provided for. Equally, it could have just been the completely different lifestyles of London and the quiet backwaters of Pembrokeshire, the former being completely alien to me.

At Brands Hatch I was in my element. The tinny sound of commentary voices booming through the loudspeakers interspersed with the deafening roar of the supercharged petrol engines thundering by, trumped a designer handbag on any day of the week. What a way to spend a weekend, walking around fast cars, loud engines and watching the thrill of racing. I met more of Dean's friends and saw him present prizes in a few of the classes he had sponsored.

I had entered a completely different world but what was there not to like about it?

I had the perfect balance between my children and a personal life while retaining my security and independence. Weekends were no longer boring; one weekend a motor show, the next outdoor pursuits. There was always something planned to look forward to and it was like I had a new lease on life.

As the months passed, we discussed coming to my home to meet my family and decided the best time would be a Sunday evening at the end of one of our weekends. As the girls came bounding through the front door he was leaning up against the cooker, facing them.

'Hello girls, it's lovely to meet you at last, your beautiful mum has told me a lot about you both.'

Their faces lit up and his words seemed to have the effect of a magic spell, they warmed to him immediately. He chatted and interacted with them so well and I could tell that he truly had kids of his own. I had not met his children as he explained the divorce was acrimonious and as a result the girls were not in the best place to meet someone new. I totally understood this as had I been in the same position with my children, this meeting would not have taken place. On this same visit, he met my parents and again, the verdict was the same.

He seemed a nice, genuine guy.

11

Mixing with Millionaires

My career was progressing well, and I had recently been appointed to be a Police Federation Representative. The Police Federation is a staff association representing all rank up to and including chief inspector. Dyfed Powys had representatives within each rank, and I was a sergeant's rep in Pembrokeshire. This would involve supporting and advising officers when required, depending on what specialism you were trained in, but it was not a job for the faint hearted. You had to be prepared to speak up, often challenging the management on Division and looking out for the interests of your colleagues which, at times, could be quite confrontational.

I had successfully been approved to be trained to represent officers in the aftermath of a firearms incident. If an officer discharged a weapon, my role would be one of support and to make sure what was requested of them by the investigating team, was lawful and necessary. In simple terms I would look after their interests at a time when they would not be able to make rational decisions themselves. My experience with firearms was limited, but I knew a fair bit about operational procedure in my role as a sergeant. I had also successfully passed a firearms assessment some time before, where I discovered I was a pretty good shot and understood what was expected in the role. I had a good solid grounding.

The course took place in London and coincided, at the end of that week, with a weekend with Dean. As I listened to the seminar my phone vibrated silently in my pocket.

Hey babe we will have to postpone this weekend.
Really? Why what's up?
You will need time to pack and check your passport. As you are on leave next week, we are flying out to Italy to the Cosmoprof trade show, couple of days away. I've got your ticket and the hotel is booked.

I raised my eyes back to the seminar with a broad smile. Who on earth would not be happy to receive a text message like that, I felt so lucky!

A quick couple of phone calls during the break allowed me to rearrange the girls' weekend and Italy was well and truly happening.

Cosmoprof is a big event on the beauty calendar. There were a few others attending this show, amongst them Dean's mogul partner and his wife. We met them in the arrivals lounge at Bologna airport while waiting for the luggage to arrive on the carousel. The partner was a smartly dressed man with glasses, thin and tall in stature. He was accompanied by his younger, head-to-toe designer-clad wife. She was dressed in a fur coat, perfectly pleated trousers and Louis Vuitton trainers.

I, on the other hand, opted for a white t shirt, jeans and a pair of white Converse flats.

Her hair was immaculately blow-dried into sleek bouncy waves while mine was frizzed up from a shower of rain that soaked me as I boarded the plane. I had tied it back with a 99p, sparkly bobble. The only thing in common between us was that we both breathed the same air.

They were pleasantly spoken but clearly on a different wavelength to me. Her days were filled with shopping and beauticians and his minding his successful business empire. I chased after villains and was verbally abused on a daily basis while supervising my team of mostly men, huddled together in a transit van on nights, sharing our chips together.

My life was one of practicalities and resolving problems. Designer items were not practical both in terms of affordability and use.

As they talked all things business, I watched the suitcases appear on the carousel, rumbling out like an army convoy. Whilst they had an assistant to collect theirs, I got myself into the scrum ready to drag my suitcase off before it did another lap around the circuit.

I watched the assistant heave their bags on to the trolley. All brown leather matching Louise Vuitton, and there were at least six. I did a mental calculation in my head and found myself, yet again, swearing in amazement under my breath at the value of that one trolley load.

All the bags had come through and the belt soon became deserted.

'Any sign of yours yet babe?' Dean asked.

'No, they must have saved the best till last,' I said, and as the belt gave one last churn, it spat out my case from behind the plastic curtains. My large, battered and bruised, bright violet case moved slowly into view.

I loved my case. It was the one the girls took on school trips and it had made many a weekend journey with me, even though it was worn and very bright.

I could feel designer eyes rolling with disbelief as I yanked it off the belt and proudly pulled up the extended handle, as if it were something for them to envy, so that I could use wheel mode.

As we walked toward the taxi bay the poor assistant was struggling to push his heavy load piled high with the precious small fortune and I noticed the beads of sweat glistening on his forehead as he focused on struggling to keep the wheels of the rickety airport trolley in a straight line.

I couldn't resist. 'Bet you wish you were pulling this little beauty instead?' I smugly announced with a smile, wink and a nod to my obedient budget case trundling with ease behind me on the smooth polished floors.

The flushed face assistant looked at my case longingly and then back at his designer pile of suitcase cash and raised his eyes. His responding wry smile needed no words.

Italy was beautiful. Bologna had a bridge over the river where we ate delicious Italian ice cream. The shops were full of real leather goods, smelling so appealing and pungent it made them almost edible.

We took a packed train to the show each day and while some complained that the lack of seating was unacceptable, we were content to cuddle, or as we say in Wales 'cwtch' up in the doorways of the carriages. We were like kids, laughing, joking and oblivious to the world outside our own space.

I met representatives of the brands mentioned on the Guvnor website. There were a few hours where Dean was engaged in meetings, so I wandered around, happy in my own company and enjoying the show. When he returned to meet me, a little later than scheduled, he was most apologetic.

'Okay Jill, tonight we are meeting the mogul and his wife as we have a meal booked with some of the QVC channel presenters who are over for the show. We will be going to this beautiful little restaurant; I am sure you will love it.'

'Of course, sounds lovely,' I said.

And love it I did.

Set on a spotlessly clean side street, as I walked through the door the smell of freshly filtered coffee meandered its way to my senses. There was an expensive looking glass counter to my left, with regally placed jars of giant pears poached in red wine. These jars were surrounded by champagne bottles, lined up on silver trays drenched in their ice cold coats. To my utter amazement, these bottles were collected by the waiters and strategically placed upon our long table. It was covered in a crisp white tablecloth and meticulously laid for sixteen guests.

I sat between the mogul and Dean and as I did so, guests started to arrive to take their places at the table. I recognised a few from television and I confess that I was a tiny bit star struck.

What the hell was a police sergeant from Pembrokeshire doing with all these stupidly wealthy people from a different planet?

My thoughts attempted to ground me.

I was literally lost for words and spent most of the evening simply listening to business talk which had little relevance to me. Regardless, I joined in with polite conversation.

Dean constantly involved me and was warm and attentive, sensing my unease.

'Madam, your starter …'

'Oh, it's okay thank you, I didn't order a starter.'

I rarely ordered a starter as I much preferred dessert and I had been eyeing the poached pear heaven from the moment I set foot in the restaurant.

'Yes, its fine,' Dean interrupted and ushered the waiter to put the plate down before me. 'I've ordered for you.'

Then quietly in my ear, 'I hope you don't mind; you were chatting.'

'Oh, okay then, no it's fine, umm… what is this?'

There was too much going on to make further objection

'Fried lambs brain, Madam, enjoy.'

Silence.

'Dean,' I whispered, 'What the hell is this? Is this really a brain?'

'Just try it darling, you will love it,' he replied, laughing and tucking into the same on his plate.

I sat with the steam wafting up into my face while simultaneously trying to casually push the plate out of view and stop myself from heaving. I left it, untouched.

Next came main course and never before had I been so happy to see a cheese and tomato or 'Margherita pizza,' as the other guests corrected me. Its extortionate price tag and my current setting and company made the official, formal title, far more appropriate.

The champagne was flowing as the serving staff ran around looking after our every need. It was not a big restaurant; it was more exclusive and a quick glance at the menu and its prices confirmed that.

Desert arrived and the giant red wine pear made my mouth water. The sweet juice cascaded like a waterfall of syrup and I demolished this at my usual high speed, a habit of my job as there was never time to eat other than on the run between calls. I was mistress in the art of speedy consumption.

As I finished, the others were still on their 'gelato', in my world 'ice cream, and the conversation remained on profit, loss, figures and wealth management.

As I sat half listening, I could feel one of the false nails on my forefinger becoming loose and I kept using my thumb to subconsciously fiddle with it.

Conversation was in full flow when I lifted my hand to take a sip from my champagne glass. It was at that exact moment that everything seemed to move in slow motion. I opened my fingers to grasp the flute and, as I did so, my forefinger flicked the side of the glass with a muted tap. The soft pink coloured nail sprang off my finger and launched skyward before arcing and heading downward. It reminded me of watching sycamore seeds or 'helicopters' as I called them, descend softly in Autumnal slow motion, gently settling on the woodland floor. But there was no gentle descent here, this was a crash landing, straight into a mountain of pink 'gelato' and cream on the plate of Mr Mogul sat beside me. I was mortified.

The good news was nobody had noticed but the bad news was his shiny dessert spoon was heading in the nail's direction.

Tell him, quick, warn him! No don't warn him, say nothing, oh God sit on your hands, sit on your hands, he may soon be full and won't eat it, he won't even notice, keep calm. My thoughts were racing.

The conversation suddenly came to an abrupt stop as Mr Mogul started choking and fishing around in his mouth with his expensively ringed finger.

Too late.

'What the blazes is this in my desert?'

The whole table looked in his direction as he lifted my nail in the air. 'It's a bloody fingernail in my gelato that is disgusting. Totally unacceptable!'

It is clean, I thought. Honestly! Keep sitting on that

hand girl.

'Waiter, here now please,' he clicked his fingers with authority, 'I demand to see the owner.'

The waiting staff were like headless chickens, frantically trying to locate him.

Then a public inspection of all the waitress's nails followed. It was like a scene from Cinderella except the burning question was, who was the owner of the nail as opposed to the glass slipper? The whole time I remained sat on my hand, it was the longest and most painful interrogation scene I had ever witnessed in my career.

Having drawn a blank, the bill was called, and dessert was obviously knocked off. I remember the mogul studying the bill as he was clearly picking up the tab. I looked over his shoulder and spotted the bottom line. Jesus H Christ, it was over two thousand euros! I looked at Dean and mouthed, 'two grand'. Dean shrugged his shoulders as if to say, 'so what?'

I was gobsmacked, I could not comprehend that amount of money being spent on a night out, let alone on just food and drink.

This truly was a different world.

Walking back to the hotel I had to cleanse my guilty conscience to Dean, it just wasn't in my nature to lie and he fell about laughing as I confessed.

'That is exactly why I have fallen in love with you, you are so not like all this bullshit, you are real and that is what I have lacked in my life until now.'

The following morning at breakfast we kicked each other like naughty children under the table as we were told the restaurant owner sent the whole batch of 'gelato' back to the supplier and demanded compensation for the serious breach of health and safety to his customers.

In the meantime, I had removed the remainder of the evidence. Not one false nail remained on my fingers.

While we were in Italy, Dean had a call on his phone and didn't hide the identity of the caller when her name flashed up on the screen.

'It's my ex, I'd better take it in case it's the kids.'

We were walking back to the hotel, so I was quite happy to slow my pace and drop back to give him some privacy.

I caught the odd clip of his raised voice, the first time I had ever heard him do it. He repeated a few times, 'I'm away on business,' which confirmed that she did not know where he was and the relationship, as he had described, was not good. I was, of course, all too familiar with how toxic things can be in the process of separation and I sympathised with him.

His actions were the same as if one of his daughters was calling. He would walk away out of earshot or leave the room but again, this is normal for many people who feel more comfortable speaking in privacy. I had no reason to suspect anything untoward or that it was anyone different, other than who he said, on the phone.

Aside from that one call, the trip was a happy one and I returned even more confident that this relationship was going to be permanent, especially when we began discussing the possibility of children. Now to some this would have been a ridiculous idea. I had known him barely six months and the relationship was relatively new, but there is that expression 'when you know you just know'. I felt like we simply fitted together and even though he lived at the opposite end of the country, we began to plan how we could logistically make our relationship work. He stated he could run his office from anywhere in the UK and would be happy to work in London during the week and travel home to me on weekends. Nothing would change for me; he was happy to make the sacrifices. I simply wanted to spend as much time as I could with him having wasted so much time and heartache on past relationships. To not grab this opportunity would have been foolish and certainly no worse than putting the brakes on and unnaturally slowing what was running at top speed. I was desperate to be happy and had found that one person who brought this. I saw no harm in making a commitment.

I had always wanted a third child, having grown up with an only brother whom in my eyes was the favoured one. I felt a third child would bring better balance to my own family.

Dean, for his part, had always wanted a son, someone to call *his boy*, and, I suppose, carry on the Jenkins line.

We made the conscious decision to try for a child. Our plans to live together were not yet in place but things were going well, and I fell pregnant quickly. Sadly, I miscarried at six weeks. It was an upsetting time for me personally as it brought back the memories I fought so hard to keep locked away. By August we had a positive pregnancy test.

I decided to take a holiday to the South of France where my parents owned a holiday home. The girls and I would fly out ahead of Dean who would arrive for a few days before we returned home together.

The weather was so warm in France and with the sun on my skin and the good, healthy food I blossomed. My brother and his family also joined me and my parents, and this was a rare occasion of the family being altogether. Ordinarily it would have been something I would try to avoid.

I met Dean at the airport, and we drove back to my parents.

Dean told me he was carrying a large amount of cash, 'a couple of grand,' was how he put it, as he had completed a business deal on his way to the airport. He was concerned about keeping it safe until he could get to the bank. He was upfront about the money and having met and seen the large amounts that people in his world were paying even in restaurants, it raised no suspicion. In fact, he relayed the same story to my mum, who agreed to keep it safe for him, without further question.

12

Jam Jar

My brother, a car salesman, seemed to get on well with Dean. He was the first born and, as such, wrapped in cotton wool with nothing ever too much trouble.

When I arrived some years later, I was less well wrapped. I guess my parents had relaxed slightly having got to grips with parenthood.

I never wanted for anything and had a good upbringing but the only thing I felt I personally lacked was the same amount of love and support which my older sibling seemed to receive in excess. I sought this perceived shortfall through my Nan and, as a result, spent most of my preferred time with her over anything planned as a family. My reluctance always had the same response.

'There is something wrong with you, you are not like normal daughters.'

I wasn't sure what 'normal' was, but it certainly wasn't going missing when I was due to go on a family holiday to France, hiding out in my nan's garden shed willing them to leave without me.

Once, during an argument, my father told me that he sometimes wondered why they ever bothered having me. I never forgot this despite it being passed off as a moment of anger. In fact, it gave me some reassurance that there was nothing drastically wrong with me, I was just simply reacting to circumstances that propelled me to search and chase the love I so desperately needed.

So, my brother, knowing Dean was a London businessman and he being a car salesman, put his selling skills into overdrive and it wasn't long before he sold Dean his car, a light blue Jaguar that he had been looking to sell. I was not happy with this as by now I wasn't a fan of mixing business with pleasure as I feared that if something were to go wrong with the car it would cause added and unnecessary friction on both sides, with me caught in the middle. The sale went ahead, regardless.

Dean was becoming more of a fixture and with his support, my own girls around me and our child on the way, I was completely happy and content.

In late September 2006, my routine pregnancy blood tests came back as a high risk for Downs syndrome. I didn't want to have an intrusive test as it carried too great a risk of miscarriage, so I paid to have what was called a 'nuchal' test in Bristol. This scan measured the amount of fluid behind the baby's head and thus gave a more accurate probability for Down's. To be perfectly honest, the test result either way would not have resulted in a termination of the pregnancy, our child was so wanted and loved. It was more for my peace of mind, and to keep my stress levels as low as possible. We travelled to the test together and the results were within the normal range. The pregnancy and our lives were progressing well.

We discussed the future and Dean decided that he would move to Pembrokeshire, with a goal set for January 2007, three months before my due date.

At work, I was moved on to restrictive duties, away from the risk of the front line what with my ever-expanding bump on my small frame. I made one of my last planned weekend visits to stay with Dean near his mum's place in Slough on the last weekend of October.

During the day we spent time together but had to go to the local garage where the Jaguar that Dean had bought from my brother had been found to have mechanical issues. I felt awful about this, but Dean assured me he would sort it out with my brother directly as he still had a final instalment to pay on the car. We arrived at the garage and walked into the side office which smelled of oil and stale coffee.

'I will leave you to it, the smell is making my stomach turn a little.'

I walked back into the yard to chat with his mum.

Five minutes later Dean reappeared. His face was stern, the lines on his forehead prominent as he frowned.

'Ready?' I asked

'No, there is a problem. I have left my wallet at mums and the bill is pretty high for the repairs. I will need to leave it here and come back Wednesday as the garage is shut until then after today. I bloody need the car for work this week...fucks sake.'

I felt awful. He had bought the car in good faith and what a surprise, there were issues!

My ever-predictable brother. 'Don't worry, I have my credit card with me, how much do you need?'

'No Jill,' Deans mum chirped up, 'don't you be paying anything, Dean will sort this.'

'Ah, its fine,' I replied 'Dean, how much?'

'It's £2,850.'

'It's what?'

'£2,850, the car was fucked.'

'Okay, its fine. I will sort this now; I am so sorry Dean.'

'Babe, it's not your fault and don't worry I will send

the cash to you this week, I just need to get my wheels back today.' He laughed. 'It's not as if I'm going to leave the country or anything.'

'Yes, its fine,' I replied and went into the office, paid the bill and returned clutching the keys.

That evening we went to a family dinner to celebrate a birthday and had a lovely time.

We said another one of my hated goodbyes on Sunday and I drove home, this time in his D7GUV jaguar, thinking how life couldn't really get much better.

Little did I know that the next time I would see Dean would be around two months later but prior to that, my life was about to get a whole lot worse.

13

No Man's Land

As Chief Superintendent Amphlett's car pulled away from my driveway, I watched from the kitchen window, gripping the edge of the cold slate worktop so hard that my fingers hurt. I felt the sharp pain from the uneven edge as I squeezed with all my strength. I just needed to confirm whether I was as devoid and empty of feelings as I believed I was. There was just one thing that my fingers and heart managed to transmit to my brain: raw pain. I felt like an empty vessel, all those warm feelings of happiness, love and contentment had disappeared like a sunset, leaving me wrapped in a cloak of chilling darkness. There was nothing left, a tornado had ripped through my very being, wreaking irreparable damage and utter devastation.

Just a few days ago, life had been pretty much perfect, but now the future had been cruelly ripped away from me with no explanation and certainly no solution.

As I stood there, I remembered an occasion when I had booked someone into custody who had been arrested on suspicion of the murder of his wife. There had been a domestic incident at the family home which had escalated out of control and, as a result, she had tragically died of her injuries.

The man had stood before me, head bowed. When he raised it to speak, his eyes were like two hollows filled with sadness, his voice soft with a fragile tone as if, like his heart, it was about to break and pour out of him in a river of emotion.

I recalled watching him. His twisted face. Momentarily drawn in to his sad and desperate predicament. Despite having apparently killed his wife, albeit in a flash of red mist, I realised that for him, life as he knew it, was over. His actions, whatever drove them over a simple period of minutes, had catastrophically changed his life forever. And for everyone in his circle. His wife was dead. Her parents had lost a daughter. His children suddenly had no mum and shortly no dad. And he would lose his home, his job, his family and spend the majority of the rest of his life behind bars.

Total devastation in the blink of an eye.

I wondered how the hell anyone could ever process or deal with this, let alone come to any terms with it. I returned home that night saddened, moved and somewhat disturbed by what I had witnessed and thankful for the life I had which although it hadn't been easy at times, it was certainly on the up.

Standing there I wondered whether Chief Superintendent Amphlett was now driving away, as I had once done, thinking those very same thoughts as I had once thought about my prisoner. I was now in the same shoes as him except that my circumstance had been brought on by the actions of another. I had not killed anyone; in fact, I hadn't done anything wrong. Yet, overnight, my personal life, my family, my home and my job had been blown apart by an incident detonated 321 miles away in a New Romney Building Society, the aftershock travelling far further than could ever be imagined.

My parents had arrived at my house that morning and it wasn't long before they began to take over.

Mum: 'Did you not have any idea that he was up to something?'

I suppose my mum was always going to ask me the obvious question first, and in my mind my sarcastic thoughts leaped into action: Well, he did mention he did a bit of armed robbery on the side but he told me not to mention it to anyone, so I didn't.

It always fascinates me how victims think and behave when in a state of shock, how the mind works, and the coping mechanisms engage. In my line of work a sick sense of humour kicked in at an early stage. I would often find myself coming out with what would seem to be an inappropriate one-liner or misplaced humour. This was a 'code' only understood and reciprocated by colleagues, but to the outside lay person would be considered unprofessional and cruel. But it was just that. A coping mechanism.

I recall a tragic road accident I attended one night on a near-deserted country road where the driver had been hurled from his vehicle and in the process was decapitated. His head came to rest on a nearby gatepost. It was a terrible scene, almost surreal, and was the first thing that caught the headlights of the police vehicle as we arrived. I recall looking at the naive, shocked young constable next to me and touched his arm. 'Are you okay, do you want to take some moments in the car?'

'No, sarge, I'm okay. How do you learn to cope with this?'

'I don't think you ever do, life is so cruel at times, and you have to try and switch off your personal emotion so you can redirect it to do the very best for the victim and the families. But we are human, and your reaction is completely normal'. I squeezed his arm reassuringly and smiled sympathetically. I had once been where he was.

'Right come on, I'm going to have you running around like a headless chicken on this one. I hope you are not afraid of the dark!'

He smiled, took a deep breath and his training kicked in. My response had lifted the overpowering urge to be overcome by the sadness of the situation and reset his professionalism button. It's so hard dealing with such extraordinary things and sometimes extraordinary measures are required to do so.

Equally as bewildering is how those who are not the victim, question and expect rational answers, as if that person is in a perfectly ordinary state of mind. Like my mum. She knew how devastated I was but seemed to expect me to deliver the normal response she would perhaps receive in an ordinary everyday circumstance. She was clearly mortified by this unexpected and unwelcome revelation of events. My parents lived quiet respectful lives in a small town. This news was devastation. I knew that.

I raised my eyes and responded to her initial question. 'Do you really want me to answer that?'

'Well, there is no need to be rude Jill, this is terrible. What on earth are people going to say down here, Pembrokeshire is a small place, and this is terrible shame to bring to our door.'

There were probably a lot of things I needed at that time, but a lecture on shame and how other people felt was not top of my list. Neither was an argument, so it wasn't long before I assured them I was fine and needed some space and it would be best for them to leave me alone.

'We will collect the girls from school, you will come to us for food tonight.'

'I don't want food, I'm fine.'

'It's not a choice Jill, your dad will pick you up at 5pm. Now have a shower and get dressed we will see you later.' And with a quick kiss on the cheek they were gone.

The house was silent, like a lull before the inevitable storm.

I shuffled about that day in my pyjamas, still attached to my phone in the deluded hope I would hear something from Dean.

Later, as arranged, my father came to collect me. I threw on some joggers, a hoodie, brushed my teeth and splashed cold water over my face and followed him, childlike, to the car.

'Come on, what's the matter with you, you have a face like a wet weekend.'

Oh, nothing really, just the small matter of my boyfriend in the slammer for armed robbery. My career has been dragged into the mix. I'm sixteen weeks pregnant and falling into the deepest black hole you could ever imagine, but other than that, Dad, I'm fucking fine.

'I'm just not hungry, Dad.'

'Come on cheer up, Mum has told your brother the news. He's on his way down from Cardiff.'

Great.

'The girls are at the house,' he continued, 'they are worried about you so don't let on anything is wrong.'

I had managed to sit the girls down and explain from the outset what had happened but assured them it would not affect their lifestyle in any way. We would still live at our home, attend the same schools and nothing would change other than Mummy being a little upset at times. At that point, I genuinely didn't know what the future held but it was so important to make them feel assured and safe.

'Nanny says you may lose our baby with all the stress,' Ella innocently piped up.

'Nanny is wrong my darling, the baby is fine, and you have nothing to worry about.'

At that moment I was inwardly furious with my mother. I suppose she was trying to prepare the way for the worst-case scenario as she knew the weight of the stress I was under but for me, it felt like a lack of support and another crutch taken away.

Relations between me and my parents became more strained. Dinner was one-way traffic. While my girls played in the living room, I underwent more interrogation followed by what felt like a well-intentioned tactical briefing in the dining room, courtesy of my parents and brother.

I recall very little, pushing the food around my plate and giving one-word answers.

They began to arrange outings, the first of which would start the following weekend. A shopping trip to McArthur Glen outlet in Bridgend. It would be lovely my parents said, and it would apparently do me good to get out.

A shopping trip was not going to free me from the prison my mind was incarcerated in, but I didn't have the strength or inclination to object. I allowed them to carry on as if I was ten years old again with no option but to do as I was told. It was just easier that way.

I recall the car journey up, I had very little to say.

Dad looked at me through the rear-view mirror, I must have looked a miserable object. 'Cheer up Jill, bloody hell what is the matter with you? We are going to meet your brother, so you'd better put a smile on that face and stop making the day miserable for everyone else.'

But I didn't smile. Quite frankly, I didn't care. I felt that I was being ushered back to reality and normality as fast as they could muster, as if that would make all of the mess and heartbreak go away.

The consensus was that the sooner Dean Jenkins disappeared from my life, the sooner life could get back to normal.

But, of course, it wasn't that simple.

When you are in a relationship, you are blinkered

to an extent. If somebody tells you somebody is no good for you, unless you are mentally and emotionally ready to come to that conclusion yourself, they may as well continue until they are blue in the face, it won't make a blind bit of difference. You may well eventually see the light, but it has to be at your pace. And human nature has always been to want what you cannot have.

'Jill, he's an armed robber for goodness sake, and you were part of his kick,' said my brother at one point in an attempt to make me ´snap out of it.' 'They shot at the police, a man is dead and why you would even want to set eyes on him again is beyond me.'

The number of times people said that to me was countless, but they were not in my shoes and could not even come close to comprehending how I was feeling.

Meanwhile, back at the police station, the wheels of investigation rumbled into motion.

Within days, Chief Superintendent Amphlett was back in touch and explained that Kent Police, the investigating force, had been appraised of the situation. They had no idea of my existence. I had been appointed a liaison officer, DC Johnston, to keep me updated with developments in Kent. He assured me they would keep my presence as quiet and as unobtrusive as possible.

I had nothing to hide but I knew as part of any thorough investigation they would need to look at me and clarify that fact for themselves. I told Kent I would cooperate without question, but doubted I had anything of value to help them. Meantime close colleagues were told what had happened and their reaction was one of total disbelief. There was, of course, the usual wave of rumours, but I wanted to make sure that those I was close to at that time heard it from me directly. I faced people head on. I felt like I had something to apologise for even though the reality was to the contrary.

Up to this point I had felt supported by the force in terms of allowing me back to work, but there was no emotional support whatsoever. I had returned to work a few days after the news of Dean and probably, in hindsight, a little too quickly. I needed a change of scenery from the endless haunted corridors in my mind. I also felt my job needed to take priority as I was frightened for my future. As such I threw myself into everything that came my way to please my superiors.

14

Knock Knock

By the second week of November I found myself standing before a group of firearms officers in the firearms range at police headquarters. I spoke about procedures. My role should they ever find themselves in a firearms incident where they had shot, wounded or even killed someone. I did this knowing full well that I was now connected, whether I liked it or not, to an armed Robbery in Kent. Where my partner was locked up and his mate shot dead by a member of a team. A team similar to those sat before me.

I should never have been standing there or

permitted to run this seminar, but my emotional wellbeing was not a priority to me. I believe the force should have stepped in; they should have made decisions in my best interest instead of allowing me to clumsily make my way down a path I was incapable of navigating.

Within a matter of days, I was told Kent Police needed to search my home. Superintendent Amphlett explained that he had suggested that this was conducted by Dyfed Powys officers as opposed to Kent. Quite frankly this was the worst suggestion he could ever have made as I did not want officers who knew me rifling through my personal possessions. He explained they would arrive with a warrant.

I looked at him in confusion. 'Why do they need a warrant? They can search my house with my full consent?'

'They insist they will bring a warrant, just procedure Jill.'

It was procedure, but as they knew full well, I was cooperating. It was a warning sign to me that the wolves were beginning to circle.

One of my team lived locally. I was her shift sergeant and she knew my character. She knew how I worked and, as such, she must have empathised on the nightmare prospect of police officers rummaging around in my personal space. My phone rang.

'Sarge, where are you now? I just overheard the

conversation about the warrant?'

'I know, I'm heading home now to tidy up.'

'Put the kettle on. I will be there in five minutes to give you a hand. Put your underwear drawer into a carrier bag, and I will take that with me. The last thing you want is a load of perverts examining what you wear under your uniform, you have enough to deal with.'

At that moment I laughed at this totally simple but accurate observation. I had been on countless warrants where the male officers sometimes argued over who would search the underwear drawer, the contents of which were described and ridiculed for weeks after. I had never believed that one day the tables would be turned on me.

I will never forget that small, kind gesture because she was the first person who showed any thought or consideration for my feelings as a human being. She was simply looking to minimise any potential humiliation and she went out of her way to do so.

The girls remained at my parents that evening as the officers arrived: A very low-key approach, four marked police cars, two unmarked cars and two marked transit vans converged on my home. There was a knock at the door and the warrant was thrust in my face. I sighed. 'You don't need a warrant; I give my consent.'

'Umm, sorry we have been told to execute it anyway. Do you have any guns in the house?'

Guns? Really? I felt like saying, 'Oh yes, there is a sawn-off behind the water tank in the roof.' Honestly!

And so, the house was searched. I had never really appreciated how much of a violation this felt like. My home was private, a place away from the workplace and my sanctuary. Now here they were scrutinising every last piece of paper and every accessible corner. Dean didn't live with me, had not recently been at my address, and it wasn't me who had just committed armed robbery. But they searched, rifling through my life for the incriminating evidence that they were never going to find.

Eventually, they removed a pair of Timberland boots belonging to Dean, a jacket which was in his Jaguar parked on the drive, my mobile phones and computer. I had two phones at the time as my old contract overlapped the start of my new one.

Over the months, 40 and I had crossed paths through work, often firearm incidents where he would cover the force area. He often appeared at my station. Life had moved on for us both, we had to work together, and with the passing of time, we had called a truce on the common ground of friendship. Earlier that day I had received text messages from him.

How you keeping fatty, any news?

Nothing much except my partner has gone and life is

once more in disarray

Where's he gone 2? Have u spoken since? He obviously knows you're pregnant. Easy for me to say but keep cool for the moment, he may see sense.

Hmm, just like you did. Not! Funny that isn't it? Actually, so very easy for you to say!

And the conversation was left at that but later that day, mid search at my home, another message came, and I knew word was filtering across the force. Nothing was kept under wraps for long.

What the hell has he done, why is the search team there?

Armed robbery it seems, they are taking my phones and computer, so I won't be able to reply

Fuck, you get dealt some hands girl. Don't u dare give up? You listening?

I dropped my phones into the plastic bags held in front of me and watched as the only channels of communication, in my eyes, I had left with Dean, were sealed up and labelled as exhibits.

As the convoy of police vehicles left my drive, I could see curtains twitching at the neighbours' houses.

I closed the door, closed my eyes and took the deepest of breaths.

The following few days I became robotic. I got the children to school, collected them and cooked tea. In between, I remained in my pyjamas taking up residence on the sofa, watching the TV with a glazed look, not really registering anything but appreciating the background noise as a non-confrontational form of company. I didn't want to communicate with anyone, answer the landline or have any interaction with the outside world. It came to the point that I had a code in place with my mum so she would ring twice, hang up then immediately ring again which meant it was safe to answer.

I felt like I was clinging precariously onto the walls of a giant black pit which were coated in thick black grease, trying to keep my grip but every day slowly descending a little bit further, sliding down by my fingernails. I wanted to sink, I wanted to reach the bottom so I could just remain there in peace with no emotional changes, but the walls would not let me.

Every day something new materialised and I couldn't deal with it. I wanted to land in the dark box and stay there until I was ready to open the lid.

That same week, Kent officers arrived at my home, where I was to answer some questions. One was a portly man with a large round belly that looked like it was trying to escape his shirt, stretching the buttons to their limit. He was dressed in typical CID attire, drab raincoat and drab suit.

The Police Federation is a statutory staff association for police constables up to and including the rank of chief inspector. All forty-three forces in England and Wales have a branch called the Joint Branch Board (JBB), and it's purpose is to represent the interests of police officers in all aspects of work: pay, pensions and, importantly, legal assistance.

Peter Dickenson was the chair of the force JBB and a colleague whom I'd known for years. We worked together when I had been stationed in Tenby, before my marriages, and now our paths crossed again through federation work. He was a very thorough police officer and took his duties within the federation very seriously. This sometimes made him unpopular with management, when he challenged the attempted introduction of unethical policies, like a new shift rota or overtime rule. He had a strong sense of integrity and hated dishonesty or unfairness. He was brilliant at his job and my first choice to support and represent me.

I was not in any fit state to make decisions. With a progressing depression and pregnancy, my hormones and emotions were in overdrive. I didn't even realise that I needed advice as I felt I had nothing to hide. I was vulnerable and incapable of seeing the bigger picture or checking the accuracy of anything put to me. Peter would cover these weaknesses.

Essentially, he would be my eyes and ears, and for that I was grateful.

The meeting lasted a good hour and the mood was friendly though I was being asked questions I simply couldn't answer other than in the negative.

'So, Jill, what can you tell us about the lock ups down here?'

'Lock Ups? I'm sorry what lock ups?'

'He had keys on him when he was arrested, they look like garage type keys?'

'I don't have a garage and he definitely didn't have any lock ups down here.'

Both officers let out a long sigh

'Jill you need to think about this. This is a dangerous ruthless armed gang you are tied up with, one of them shot at police with a sawn-off shotgun and as a result was shot dead.'

'I'm really sorry but I can't tell you what I don't know.' He doesn't have anything here...no lock ups, no guns no nothing.

The Kent officers continued.

'Are you aware you weren't the only woman he was in contact with?'

'What do you mean?'

'Well, he was happily married, and we also found the numbers on his phone of women he'd been texting.'

I felt my stomach lurch.

Funny how at that time this news was more life-changing for me than the armed robbery details.

'I don't know anything about that?' I looked at Peter. 'Is that right?'

'Hang on a second now.' Peter's voice was firm. 'I don't think upsetting Jill with that sort of information right now is appropriate. I appreciate you are trying to achieve whatever goal you have, but come on now, that's out of order.'

There was a pregnant pause in the conversation, followed by another sigh. 'Okay, so where were we. Umm…okay, did he keep any guns here?'

The questions kept coming and I remembered starting to feel guilty for being unable to provide anything positive. I sensed their increasing frustration.

'Okay, we want you to make a statement.' They pulled some crisp white letter-headed statement paper from their file.

'Umm, wait a minute,' Peter interjected, 'What does she need to make a statement about? We have just heard she has nothing of use to assist you. Once she makes a statement, as you both well know, she can be called as a witness to court. You have just told us how dangerous these people are, one being the father of her child. And she is a police sergeant. I am not happy with an unnecessary statement, what about her safety? She would be thrown to the wolves both in terms of physical safety and the press.'

'Umm, well, we want a statement; we can't leave here without one.'

'No, I'm sorry, at this juncture I'm advising Jill not to make a statement and my duty is to her well-being. I will consult our chief constable for advice before we agree to do anything.'

I was so thankful to Peter. I hadn't thought further than the edge of the sofa. I certainly had not thought of the potential consequences for me. I was frightened by his words and agreed the last place I wanted to be was in a witness box.

The house was lonely when everyone had gone, but it was my preferred place to be.

My girls were with me during the days on weekends. I kept them close, suspicious of everyone around me now the word was fully out as to what had happened.

I set myself tasks, just simple ones, to try and at least appear externally 'normal'.

But each day seemed to get harder and I would wake each morning to the prospect of being immersed in the same wilderness of grief. I tried to dilute the impact of my tears and explained to my girls they were simply a normal physical reaction; it was good to cry and for them not to worry. As a result, I would sometimes find myself crying while laughing with them over something they had done. They grew to see it as just a physical reaction that needed to run its course and when it was done, Mummy would be better.

But my mind had never felt so utterly exhausted, tired of the repetitive unanswered questions and bored of myself. I tried to make sense of things by keeping a diary.

Another hard day. Tears on waking and that's all I do. My mind goes over the same questions when I'm awake-I sleep-I must sleep? Do I sleep? And then more of the same as soon as I open my eyes. I don't know truth from lies anymore, I am suspicious of everyone and have become like a frightened mouse, I don't even recognise the woman I was. He has ripped the soul from me, and I don't know how to get it back.

But life had to drag on.

Every day was bloody Groundhog Day.

15

Sawn Off

One Sunday I was in the kitchen doing some ironing when my home phone rang. I recognised the voice at the other end of the line immediately, Dean's mum. This was the first time we had spoken since the arrest.

My heart felt like it did an emergency stop and my body went numb. Finally, some answers, I thought. 'Hi, have you heard from him?'

There was no formality, I went headlong in with the burning question, but her voice sounded on edge, hesitant, as if she needed to get her words out as quickly as possible and then be gone.

'Umm, listen Jill, I begged Dean to tell you the truth about his wife, I am so sorry, but he is still married and lives at home with her and always has done. He's been leading a double life and his poor wife didn't have a clue.'

Her voice tailed off as I slid my back down the warm hallway radiator and sunk down to my knees.

She continued.

'We visited him yesterday along with Dean's sister. He's been badly beaten and says he was in a getaway car outside the back of the Nationwide while his father was a look-out a bit further away. Not that it matters but he was in the Jag Dean bought from your brother. Bob Haines has been shot dead and poor Dean, well he looks so terrible, he watched them kill Bob, Jill. The police dragged Dean from the getaway car, stamped him to the floor and wrenched his head around, he could see it all.'

His discomfort on arrest was of no interest to me and swerved my sympathy.

'Hang on now. Stop there. You are telling me he used the Jag registered to him as a look-out car?'

'Yes, but it was still registered to your brother as he'd not finished paying for it completely. Then, of course, you went and paid the repair bill on it. I'm sorry, but now we are none of us in a position to pay you back. But never mind the car, Dean looks awful.'

My mind was racing. The car he needed back for work that week. Urgently. Ah, now this makes sense, aside from who would be so fucking stupid to use a car registered to my brother as a look-out car? Or was that deliberate too?

'Has he mentioned me?'

'No Jill, he only wants his family around him. I'm sorry love, he doesn't want anything to do with you. He and his wife want to focus on themselves.'

'Does she know about me?' I interrupted her flow.

'Umm, yes but I don't want to get involved in all that. It's probably best we don't speak again. Good luck with the pregnancy and everything. I'm so sorry, I've got to go now.'

And she was gone.

Her job was done.

I replaced the receiver and felt myself slide deeper toward the bottom of that black pit. Like a lift stuck on the tenth floor, I suddenly descended at speed to level two. The strength that had been keeping me from sliding too fast, seeped from every pore of my being. Like a leak of golden brake fluid, there was no longer any safety mechanism in place. Not even tears. I was full of the most dangerous grief and had suddenly moved far beyond the confines of deep sadness.

I was entering new territory, the vast wilderness of a deserted fool.

I walked back into the kitchen and slumped over the ironing board, head in my hands, waiting for my brain to process what I had just heard: Poor Dean, he's in a terrible state. He's led a double life for the best part of a year and now he's not only been arrested for armed robbery but also his unsuspecting wife has found out about me and the baby. Poor Jill, you were just some side show entertainment and your services are no longer needed. Good luck with the pregnancy in your world of devastation, Dean is reconciling with his wife. Again, Dean is reconciling with his wife. He chooses his wife. He doesn't choose you.

I picked up the iron and finished the last school skirt. The iron hissed in protest to the tears landing on its hot, angry surface.

I suppose anyone functioning in a sane dimension would have vowed to cut all contact with Dean Jenkins at this stage, but I was pregnant with his child and I wanted answers as to how someone could treat another human being so cruelly. Had he brutally betrayed me? Did he ever love me? Was the wife situation all true? I wanted the answers from him, and I wanted to see his face as he gave them. I was owed that much. I couldn't just walk away; we were tied for life with my pregnancy.

A couple of senior officers had considerately suggested I may be better terminating the pregnancy which would in turn protect my future career prospects, making a clean break from Dean. General off the cuff comments 'What will you do with the pregnancy?' progressed to a full-blown conversation.

One male inspector broached the subject while enquiring into my welfare. 'How is the pregnancy?'

'It's all fine, thank God,' I replied while protectively placing my hand over my perfectly formed football size bump.

'Hmm, thing is, it's not going to do your career prospects any good long term; baby whose father is an armed robber and you a police officer? Something has to give?'

I looked at him. 'Meaning what exactly?'

'Well, you are not too far gone to make some decisions which long term would safeguard your career.'

I was furious. 'With respect SIR, I will pretend you never made such a typically male, thoughtless and inappropriate comment and this conversation is over.' As I walked away, I felt the anger rise within me, like a volcano about to belch its molten anger from within its hidden depths and bury everything in its path.

I was a mother protecting my child. Who the hell did these people think they were?

I was horrified by this suggestion and at the audacity to try and dictate my personal circumstances. My pregnancy was very much planned, wanted and loved and they could take everything else from me in my professional life, but not my child.

I would not be making the same mistake twice.

Peter understood how I felt, and it was agreed with the chief constable that I could send a letter to the prison where Dean was now incarcerated to see if there was any response. Within a week, the first correspondence dropped through the letterbox, a small brown envelope with a prison number scrawled on the back. I sat and looked at the unopened envelope for some time before I had the courage to tear open the rough, cheap brown paper.

Dear Jill,

I got your letter. Thank you. It's good to hear you and the baby are well and, on the 4th December you will know what it will be, not too long now for you to wait as patience never was a strong point of yours.

I want to make clear Jill and as you are probably fully aware knowing me as you do that I would like to be informed about the little one as much as possible.

There are many things in my mind regarding us and nothing I would put on paper right now, but if you know me like I think you do, you know what's in my mind.

There are so many things I am sorry for, firstly putting you through this mess and the complete humiliation for you, I am truly sorry for that. Yes I was at home with my family but was never there, always out, or at yours or even staying at my work some nights if the truth be known. So in many ways I lived what I preached. I only ever told that one lie to you, however will understand if you never want to hear my name again. If you want to write to me and keep in touch that would be nice but I am not sure if you can due to your work circumstances which is why Jill I never got in touch before. My trouble is the last thing you need around your neck.

I am sure people have painted all kinds of pictures about me and my life and money etc, a lot of it is to protect everyone. Think about it and you will understand.

Please let my family take the Jag back after the police release it, I need to pay you back and nobody has it at the moment.

Take Care all four of you,

Dean xx

But his troubles were around my neck and the noose was getting tighter. Most days I felt I couldn't breathe; my whole body was being stifled by everything brought upon me and there was simply nothing I could do to stop it.

The Jag was obviously part of the investigation, I learned that it had been spotted acting suspiciously near the New Romney building society weeks before the robbery took place. Clearly staking out the job. I also learned Dean's dad had been a special constable at some point and had worked as a security officer on the very sort of van they had attacked. I didn't need to be a genius to work out how valuable the information he brought to the party was.

And again, I had met his dad and he had come to stay at my house one weekend with Dean. A quiet, warm man who had not been well, having had heart problems and looked like he couldn't run a mile let alone hold up a bank and make off with the cash.

In one weekend I now realised I left two parts of a four-man armed gang sat on my sofa eating cake while I commenced an eight-hour shift in a sleepy Pembrokeshire town with a remit to prevent crime.

How on earth does anyone make any sense of that?

I slowly began to realise I had been part of a double life enacted to perfection. Was it truly a life he craved? Or was it a huge joke on my behalf? I couldn't answer that but what I did know was that the first life was kept so well away from me that I had no suspicion anything was amiss. He had not lied to me; he had just been extremely economical with the truth. I never asked and was simply never told. But it was almost laughable, why would a police sergeant randomly ask her partner, a businessman, whether he spent his weekends fitting in an odd armed robbery? It was ludicrous and would not have crossed the mind of even the sanest of people.

Peter approached my chief constable at the time, Terry Grange. He was a nice, straight man and would be brutally honest regardless of whether people liked it or not. I had the greatest respect for him. CC Grange sent me an email stating he had no objection to me visiting Dean in prison, as long as Peter accompanied me for support.

16

From Prison to Maternity and Beyond

The first visit took place in December when I was five months pregnant. We drove to Elmley prison on the Isle of Sheppey, an eleven-hour round trip. I had been to prison plenty times before to interview inmates regarding outstanding crimes, but never on a personal level. As we drove down the long driveway the high grey concrete walls covered in rolls of barbed wire looked like the gates to hell, cold and uninviting, exactly as they were designed to look. I shivered at the thought of anyone I loved being incarcerated behind them.

I followed the prison officer toward the security

area with around ten other visitors. Loud, uncouth women with miniskirts, thigh-length boots, dark-rooted yellow bleached hair and cheap fake fur bolero jackets. Some were dressed to give their eagerly waiting partners the sexual testosterone fuelled thrill, of the female kind, that prison life restricted. They contrasted sharply with smartly dressed older couples, their faces weary and lined from the strain, shame and circumstance of what family members had brought upon them.

I was body searched before the sniffer dog checked me out and finally walked through a human metal detector into a large, stuffy room, set out somewhat like the local job centre office, but on a grander scale. Small tables were screwed to the floors with hard orange seats jutting off them like a children's ride at the fairground. Except there was no fun to be had here.

In the corner, a cafeteria functioned like it was on a local high street somewhere in normal land.

I would not describe myself as proud by any means, but I watched the people filing into the room and felt out of place and awkward. Some of them behaved like this was a random family day out, the kids high fiving the guards and tugging at their mothers coats to buy sweets. Laughter. And there were so many visitors, I felt my forehead furrow as I tried to think about anything remotely sane or funny about where I was sitting. I half expected Dean to appear dressed as a camp game show presenter in a white sparkly suit, cheesy smile and shackled to the knees, proclaiming 'A mere joke, folks! Just a huge, elaborate joke!'

The door opened and he walked towards the table, grey tracksuit joggers, sweatshirt, wearing a coloured bib like a netball player. He opened his arms to hug me, but I swiped them away as if they were an irritating fly. He sat down.

His voice was low 'Hey, how you doing?'

More stupid questions. 'I'm still breathing Dean, that's about the only thing left that I can do without humiliation or pain.'

'I am truly sorry about all this.'

'Oh, that's alright then! You are truly sorry about being a law-abiding citizen with no involvement with the police, to the next minute being part of an armed gang robbing banks with sawn-off shotguns. Are you also as truly sorry for dating a police sergeant while apparently robbing this bank, planning a life and child with her while all the time your wife is home with her two children, thinking you are at work?' My voice was low but I spat the words out like poison.

'I only asked Mum to tell you all that stuff to distance myself from you as I knew you were getting shit from your job; you know how I feel about you.'

'Shit from my job? What the fuck do you expect I am going to get? I am a police sergeant for Christ's sake! And, you know what, I don't know anything anymore. So much deceit. The damage is done Dean, how could you do what you've done knowing I was pregnant? Why did you allow things to progress so far between us? You have blown my life apart!'

He looked at me, expressionless and his eyes seemed to glaze. 'Because I love you.'

The dagger in my heart twisted. 'You don't destroy people you love Dean.'

'I didn't mean to; I didn't know I would fall for you the moment I saw you. I just wanted enough money to leave this fucking fake life up here and come down to you, that's all. Please Jill, we have a baby coming, I am likely to be here for a long time, time will pass, and we can make a life together, you will have retired by then. I didn't mean this to happen, my marriage was dead and has been for so long, and my life so lonely until there was you.'

'I fell in love with you Dean, you became my whole world and we had a future, or so I thought. But it was an illusion, it was what I wanted it to be, not reality. Trouble is love is love and it doesn't play well with common sense. I wish I could hate you but I'm so lonely, I'm lost and I feel like I'm battling the world because everything I knew has gone. You, my family, warmth. My world is like walking through a black, charred forest, I walk the same path daily and nothing changes. Nothing grows. It's so cold. You've destroyed me.' I looked up and saw the prison officers were watching me. I wiped my streaming eyes in shame and passed the back of my hand across my runny nose. I tried to re set myself, straightening myself up. 'I don't know what will happen Dean, I came here only by consent of my chief. I'm a bloody sergeant in the police and you, no doubt, are soon to be a convicted armed robber and we have a child on the way. Two worlds have collided and not just collided: it's been like a bloody nuclear explosion. Neither world can ever be the same again.'

'Please Jill, if you only hear one thing, it's that I love you. I have only ever tried to protect you. My marriage is dead, everyone knew that. This is why they all loved and welcomed you into the family. I've been stupid and I will pay the price for that gladly, but none of the stuff about you is lies. It was real and it is real.'

'And how am I supposed to believe that? I don't believe a word anyone says to me anymore, and that is not a great place to be.'

'I know that, but in time you will see, I will get the divorce I will prove that in all this mess I love you.'

'Is that why you are having visits from your wife? Silence.

'Because, apparently, according to your mum, you are rebuilding your marriage and have plans for a happy ever after? That, along with the countless other women you were in contact with, according to Kent Police.'

'As I said, that was to distance you from all of this shit. There was only ever you, they are lying to you Jill.'

'Oh yes, silly me, of course they are. It seems everyone likes to lie to me Dean, I'm good for that at least.'

The bell rang and the visit was over.

I left with a summary in my head, logically weighing up and trying to process what I had been told. He was only continuing to have his wife visit the prison to keep the heat off me. He loved me and everything he had ever told me was true. He was desperate. Kent Police were lying. But what about these other women? He loved me. He said he loved me.

There was something to grasp, if I needed it. But did I need it? That was the question.

On our journey home that day, a strange coincidence occurred in that Peter received a call on his mobile from Kent Police stating they wished to pay me another visit.

He automatically clicked the call onto loudspeaker so that I could hear the full conversation.

'You've already visited once,' he said. 'We are so close to Christmas I don't believe Jill is in any fit state. She needs to try and keep things as normal as she can for her and the kids.' Peter's voice was friendly but firm.

'There are things we need to put to her face to face.'

'If there are any further questions, my advice is that these are put to Jill in writing, where she can answer them with the least stress. Incidentally, all requests to her are supposed to be going through her divisional commander, not just random unexpected calls. She is not in a good place mentally.'

'Well, we would like to visit and get this over with before Christmas.'

'I'm sorry,' Peter continued, 'I have spoken to our force's Professional Standards department and they have agreed that Jill does not have to answer any more questions at this time. She will happily do so via email, but a personal visit is out of the question. She has been eliminated as a suspect and her welfare now comes first.'

Somehow, I didn't think this was the end of the matter.

It had gradually become apparent that Kent detective constables were trying to assert their authority. However, I was following the advice of my chief constable and I believed that as I couldn't go much higher up the chain of command, this was the safest thing to do as opposed to following that of a constable from an external force. Kent officers did not like this, and it began to show. I gained the distinct impression that simply because Peter was looking after my interests, they viewed this as obstruction, although I was not a suspect and had nothing of evidential value to offer them.

It seemed that as a police officer, though technically you have rights, to execute them would not be without punishment.

Unsurprisingly, less than a week before Christmas, I was told by Chief Superintendent Amphlett that the Kent detectives had prepared a new list of questions they wished to put to me, but they wanted to visit me at home to obtain the answers personally. Peter again objected but Chief Superintendent Amphlett contacted me to say that if I didn't cooperate as told, they had enough to arrest me. It was just before Christmas which would of course be, 'an awful thing for the kids at home with Mum in custody' and perhaps something I needed to consider.

But it wasn't a consideration at all. However thinly veiled or disguised, it was a threat from the organisation I had given the lion's share of my working life to.

I was angry but petrified and told Peter to put his concerns for my health aside and just agree to the meeting.

'But Jill, you are not a suspect, they have no evidence. This is a typical bullying tactic and I am not having it, look at the state you are in!'

'They will do it though, Pete, they will do it deliberately, probably on Christmas Eve and I can't and won't have the girls upset anymore. Let's just do it, we can go to HQ and get the meeting over and done with there and then.'

He took a deep breath, sighed deeply and nodded reluctantly.

Peter spoke to Chief Superintendent Amphlett and he brokered the meeting. He met me and Peter at headquarters and showed us into the conference room. He departed quickly, before the questions commenced.

There was nothing new. The questions were almost the same. I gave the same answers, it wasn't difficult as I had told the truth the first time around. I felt so tired and frustrated now with the whole repetitive process.

But there was a new question.

'Have you been to visit Dean?'

I sighed. 'Yes, but you know that already, you called within half an hour of me leaving the prison. I know I am being monitored and prison records will confirm my visits.'

'Oh well, umm…did you discuss the case?'

'I don't know much about the case and I'm not interested. My visit was for personal reasons only.'

'Well, we don't think it was wise, you visiting.'

'May I interject there?' Peter was angry, exasperated, he raised his voice a decibel or two. 'Jill is an officer of Dyfed Powys Police and her chain of command ends with Chief Constable Grange. We make it our business to run everything by him and follow his instructions. He gave permission for the visit. Your opinion is, with the utmost respect, not required.'

The police officer looked a little shocked at Peter's forthright outburst.

'Okay, point taken,' he said, 'but we would appreciate a heads-up if you happen to discuss the case with him and glean any idea of what he intends to plead.'

'She won't be discussing the case. That, as you know, would be unethical and unprofessional. Now if that is all, Jill needs to go home to her family.' Peter stood. He wasn't going to take no for an answer.

As we left, they returned my computer and phones that had been seized after the search. The computer no longer worked properly. It was running slow and I wasn't sure whether they had used some device on it which had ruined the software, or whether it was bugged. My mind opted for the latter.

I was concerned about the phones, purely because they contained pictures of my children and also, pictures for Dean's eyes only; me in a semi clad state displaying my pregnancy bump. I didn't want these in circulation, they were extremely personal, and my life was already exposed enough as it was without my half-naked body being passed around the force. I specifically asked the question, referring to the photos, as to whether any had been downloaded, circulated to my force or kept to which I was reassured nothing had. I was handed a sheet with small thumbnail pictures which I recognised from my phone.

'These are the only downloads and we are handing them back to you, as we are obliged to do. Nothing has been kept or circulated to Dyfed Powys.'

For that, I was relieved and grateful. I travelled home in the hope that I would get some peace over the Christmas period.

Dean had started calling me from the prison and the phone calls were kept strictly to my welfare. I was petrified to mention the case and did not discuss it other than to tell him how upset I was about it all and the pressure I felt was being exerted upon me by the Kent investigation team. I wanted to help them, but I couldn't make sense of anything and certainly did not have the kind of information I was sure they were hoping for.

I strangely felt some comfort in the calls from Dean.

Relations were still very strained with my family as I was not following what they believed to be the right approach to the situation. The police family were of little support and I sensed that some of them had even become almost hostile, that they had made up their minds that I must have known what had been going on.

I held on to any morsel of love or scrap of support that came my way, especially from anyone who understood how lonely I felt. Nobody had told me that I was not to have communication with Dean. The chief constable had said that long-term, as in when Dean left prison, the situation would not be tenable. If I was still in a relationship with him I would, understandably, have some decisions to make, as I could not be a police officer and in a relationship with a convicted armed robber.

To me that was almost irrelevant, yet completely understood, as it was a long way off. For the present he was locked securely inside prison where his every move was monitored. I needed time to come to terms with the situation. The chief expressed his belief that after the birth I would undoubtedly be able to think more clearly, and the relationship would naturally die a death.

Christmas came and went, and things continued in the same vain. I received telephone calls from Dean, and I visited, making the long journey whilst heavily pregnant and feeling especially vulnerable at this time. I just needed some form of comfort which he was happy to provide.

Thirteen days prior to my due date, I received a courtesy telephone call from Kent Police.

'Hi Jill, just wanted to let you know that some of your phone records evidence you calling Dean in March 2006.'

'Yes, I replied, that would be right. What of it?'

'Well, the thing is we can use this evidence to pinpoint his location in the proximity of some other robberies that he is denying. If he continues to plead not guilty to these further offences, bringing it to five in total, it is likely we will have no choice but to use you as a witness at court where, unfortunately, you name, identity and relationship will be exposed.'

I couldn't believe what he'd just said. Five in total. One had become five.

'Why would you do that? You know I want no involvement in this, please don't let this happen?'

'Well, I'm afraid it is what it is. Of course, if he well… happens… to… plead guilty to these further offences, it won't make any difference to his sentence as the judge will take his honesty into account and there is only a maximum prison term he can sentence him to anyway. Your name, most importantly, will be kept out of it and that will be the end of it.'

That evening I was devastated as the 'bonus' news sank in. More lies. *Five* robberies in total. Was he doing these since he had been in a relationship with me?

I found myself racking my brain once again in the search for any signs, but still nothing.

That night when my landline rang Dean was on the phone. 'Hey how are you doing?'

'So, Dean, not just one, but five robberies. Fucking *five*, are you serious?'

'Wait, I can explain.'

I was about to hang up and yet I wanted to hear what he had to say. 'Was it an extra kick knowing what I did for a living? They have phone records where I have been phoning you or you me, I can't remember which, which locate you near these 'extra' robberies at the time they took place. Stop your bullshit lies and tell the truth.'

'I swear, I didn't do them, they have no evidence and they are just turning the screws on you.'

'Don't tell me, oh let me guess, while you held a shotgun to someone's head you thought, *Oh, I know, let's put in a phone call to the sergeant at the same time!*' My voice was raised now and I knew I was screaming down the phone. 'Well, let me tell you something loud and fucking clear: They turn the fucking screws any which way they want but I'm telling you this, I knew nothing about any of this shit so you just do what you have to do keep me out of this. I am not going to Court, I'm due to give birth in thirteen days and if you put me through anymore of this fucking heartache, I swear to God you will never see or hear from me again.'

I didn't wait for a response. I slammed the receiver down and, yet again, tears flowed.

The next morning, still upset and shaken I contacted the then head of Professional Standards, Detective Chief Superintendent Evans. He was a tall slender man with, in my view, the look of a weathered, unfit smoker. His role was to head up his team, rooting out corrupt officers and punishing them accordingly. A difficult job, but one which he appeared to openly relish. I explained that I felt I was being used to exert pressure on Dean regarding the case, and that it was not ethical or fair to be manipulated in such a way. He stated he would send officers to take a complaint from me.

Two officers arrived, clearly for 'witness purposes'. I wasn't trusted. 'We understand you want to make a complaint against Kent police?'

'You do realise I made this complaint twelve days ago; I am due to give birth today?'

'Oh yeh, umm, sorry about that, we are busy. Nice place you got here!'

'Can we please just get this done, I feel strongly that Kent are trying to use me as a lever to Dean, to get him to take these extra charges. I don't want to be used in this way and I don't think it's ethical from his point of view either'.

'Okay, let's do a statement.'

That was the last I ever heard on that matter. I was simply a paper exercise.

Three days later Dean Jenkins appeared at Maidstone Crown Court and pleaded guilty to all five offences. He continued to deny, to me at any rate, of being involved in these extra robberies but I didn't feel thankful or pity. I was just relieved that I had dodged another bullet.

A week after my due date I went into labour. The labour ward was unusually quiet and after my son was born, I was wheeled to a six-bedded bay where we were alone. Just me and this tiny, squirming and warm perfect ball of love.

My son. Our son.

The moon was shining like huge spotlight through the big glass windows of the ward. It was unreal; a feeling of terrible loneliness mixed with a huge amount of love and protection for this tiny bundle snuggled in front of me.

I thought, 'This is the best thing you have done in a very long time, Jill. There is hope.'

I took a few a few brave steps up out of the darkness that night. I was so thankful I had something so perfect and safely delivered to live for and to protect.

And protect him I would. Always.

But for that moment, I just wanted to remain bathed and wrapped tightly in the safe blanket of love and peace that enveloped us both.

17

Daddy was a Bank Robber

The days that followed I remained encased in a warm cocoon of peace. I only had to look at Frankie, and the emotional pain of my circumstance seemed to fade, at least for a little while.

The reception to his arrival was mixed. Caitlin struggled having to share the attention and, as a result, was quite irritated by it all. She displayed little interest in her new baby brother and chose to spend more time with her dad where the attention was exclusive and money abundant. Ella, however, was in her element, helping me and loving every moment of happiness that this new tiny person brought.

I spent my days looking after the children and going for warm summer walks with the pram, the sun on my face, fresh air and birdsong like magic medicine, the simple things. It felt as if I had been sent this respite from above to recharge my flagging spirit.

It was indeed working.

My first real outing was to the Registry office, to register Frankie's birth.

The building, once an old grammar school, retained most of its original features. It had that old library smell of crisp paper and polished wood and was silent aside from the distant hum of a floor polisher, buffering the spotless white marble floors.

I was shown through to an office with rows of files and books crammed on to the wooden, floor-length shelves. A very smartly dressed registrar greeted me from behind a green leather topped desk. 'Good morning Miss Evans, do come in. May I firstly congratulate you on the birth of your son.'

I clumsily manoeuvred the pram and parked it next to the chair as she kindly ushered me to take a seat.

'I understand you are here to register the birth. Is Dad joining us today?'

'Umm no, unfortunately he won't be able to make it today.' Or any day.

'Oh okay, that's fine, you can complete the registration on your own. A few details first; your full name and occupation?'

'Jill Evans, police sergeant.'

She wrote on the thick-headed certificate with a beautiful ink fountain pen, the jet-black ink shining as it dried. 'Great and now can I have Dad's name and occupation?'

'Dean Jenkins, occupation...' Bank Robber.

'Company Director.'

'Okay, that's all done. I just need a signature from you, and Frankie is officially registered.

Let's have a look at him. May I?' I smiled and nodded as she pulled the soft blue blanket down from his face and peered into the pram. 'He is perfect. You must be very proud.'

I beamed and my heart took flight, bursting at the seams, brim-full of love.

I begrudged having to share such perfection with Dean, but my head had always been the same on this matter. I now had three children, each one had a different father but regardless of my relationship with each of the dads, it was never my place to affect their relationship with their child. My children would never be used as pawns in a point-scoring game. I had witnessed that so many times in my job and I despised it. Access would always be as full as they wanted, names on the birth certificate and their relationship the same opportunity to flourish as mine. My only insistence was that the children remained together living with me, which had always suited the dads anyway.

I resumed my position as sergeant on my Operational Response team. However, prior to taking maternity leave, I was also appointed as the sergeant responsible for the setting up and managing the Neighbourhood Policing unit. This was a relatively new concept as the force had not long commenced the recruitment of PCSO's, police community support officers, the goal being to get policing back to basics with the headline, 'Bobbies back on the beat'.

While on maternity leave, Neighbourhood Policing was officially launched and promoted to the public within Pembrokeshire in the form of a double-page newspaper article. Every member of the team was photographed with a police biography attached. I was not included in the article and was instead replaced by a male sergeant who had no involvement with Neighbourhood Policing.

I was extremely upset on how noticeable my exclusion was. I lodged a formal complaint and politely requested clarification on the matter, which culminated in a meeting with the Human Resources Manager.

'It is nothing more than you were off having a baby, so were not available for a photo,' he drawled.

I was on maternity leave with my son! I thought.

'You were in regular touch with me and I would have happily come in, but I was never asked, and was not informed about the feature. I've been replaced by a male sergeant who has had nothing to do with the development of the unit.'

'It's no big deal, we just needed a sergeant on the poster.'

'But I did the work. I've worked hard to launch the unit successfully.'

'As I said, no big deal. Now is there anything else or is that it?'

And that was the clarification delivered.

I did not feel at all valued for my work, in fact it was more a case of feeling penalised for my gender and having to take time off to give birth.

I was sent on a Neighbourhood Policing course to Carmarthen HQ. Following this, due to my domestic situation, I requested that my working hours be reconsidered to between the hours of 7.30am and 6pm, those being the times I could secure childcare for Frankie. My parents did not want to be tied to babysitting duties, after all they had done their time and raised their children, as my dad often reminded me. I was happy to be flexible, to suit the needs of the organisation, and went to the extent of formulating and submitting a few sample rotas. I did not expect the job to work around my personal life and fully understood that any sacrifices would be down to me.

A female inspector reviewed my request and approved it, stating she fully supported and understood my position and could see no detrimental effect on the organisation to what I had proposed. She submitted it to the HR department for final approval.

Within a few days, I received a response.

Refused. It would not be 'appropriate to my role.'

I loved the job I performed, very much a front-line officer and the last thing I wanted was to be stuck behind a desk. However, this was given as my only option. If I agreed to take on a brand-new role of Resources Manager, basically sat inside formulating and producing shift rotas daily, away from the front-line, then they would permit the working hours I had requested.

With little choice, I accepted.

I had no desk, chair or computer and when they did eventually provide them, it was equipment that had been piled up in the rear garages for disposal. I found myself spending hours on given tasks, only to be told on completion that other staff had already carried them out and my efforts were unnecessary.

I felt devalued but I kept my head down and kept quiet.

A few months into my new role, a male sergeant was appointed to Neighbourhood Policing and was allocated the same working hours as I had requested.

With Saturdays off to play rugby.

I was furious.

Dean was still in touch.

We had somehow settled into a pattern of phone calls and letters. I took Frankie to visit when I could, to ensure that despite what the future held for us, he had that initial bond and contact. This was my innocent son; this was not our lifestyle or how I was brought up. I had been dropped headlong into this world and I had very little choice but to continue to try and do the right thing for Frankie. I missed the Dean I thought I knew. Terribly. The loneliness he left me with had become physically painful and so that morsel of contact was like an aspirin, taking the edge off the relentless torment.

There was little correspondence during this time from Kent or Professional Standards although Peter kept a watchful eye. Outwardly I am sure I appeared fine, but inwardly I was still clinging to the side of that black hole and I felt like a puppet, in some state of suspension, waiting for the next person to play my strings.

As Dean's trial date approached, I was called to see Chief Superintendent Amphlett.

'Come in Jill, take a seat.'

'Everything okay boss?'

'Umm well, I need to inform you that a Service Confidence Procedure has been carried out on you. I can't tell you what was discussed but you have to go to Carmarthen today for a meeting with Assistant Chief Constable Edwards and the Head of Professional Standards, Chief Superintendent Evans.'

Service Confidence Procedure was a meeting conducted by senior management including Professional Standards, where the officer under scrutiny does not fall into disciplinary action or investigation but where confidence regarding the integrity of that person is in doubt.

I sighed. The rollercoaster was coming back around the track and heading in my direction.

Upon my arrival at headquarters, I entered the senior officers' suite. In a small, overheated and stuffy office, sat ACC Edwards. He was a balding man with a face as round as a full moon shining in a dark graveyard and in my opinion, equally as menacing. I had never been his biggest fan; I had quickly summed up the senior management team and I personally struggled to trust anything he said. He reminded me of a smiling assassin. Here was a man who appeared desperate to secure a Chief Constable role and who would jump through any brownie point hoop to get there.

He sat, in contrast next to the spindly-framed Chief Superintendent Evans and, as we entered, I was hit with the mixture of hot air, sweat and stale cigarette smoke.

'Sergeant Evans, we have called you here today as there are concerns about your ongoing communication with Dean Jenkins. He will shortly be before the court for sentencing and press activity will be rife. This will mean adverse publicity for the force if the relationship between you is exposed. Therefore, this is your official notification that you will now be closely monitored.'

He fiddled with his pen before he asked, 'Have you continued to visit him?'

You know the answer to that question already, I thought. 'Yes, sir, I have, nobody has ever told me I can't?'

I could hear a pencil scratching furiously on paper and shifted my eyes to Evans whose head was down, avoiding eye contact and scribbling away on a stained notepad with curled, tatty edges.

'Umm, well yes, that is correct, but we need to monitor this situation. Mr Grange's laid-back approach does not concur with mine.'

'But he is the chief constable, sir,' I interjected. 'Peter and I feel the man at the top is the best and safest advice to follow as then there can be no confusion.'

'The reputation of this force is my only priority Sergeant Evans. Therefore, you will be served with this confidence procedure notice.'

He stood up, signifying the meeting was at an end.

I gained the impression following that meeting that ACC Edwards did not warm towards me either. Peter was liaising directly with the chief constable and this did not seem to sit well with him. I felt he wanted to be top dog.

What I probably needed at that time was some strong guidance from the force. I had never been given an ultimatum and was fully aware my every move was monitored. Prison visits. Phone records. All easily obtainable. I had nothing to hide and was relieved everything was logged so there could be no confusion or suggestion of dishonesty. I was processing post traumatic shock. The chief had not forbidden the contact, so I simply continued along the track I had become used to.

Love and a career are two different things. I have seen people lose careers over love and *vice versa*. It's a tough call to make and most who make it are not of rational mind. Those eager to pass opinion on my situation had no comprehension of the hotbed of emotions bubbling through my veins, pulled back and forth like the tide and controlled by the external force of the moon. I seemed to have the option to sit on a seemingly endless fence and delay making any decision.

It was a preferred one. I knew I would have a lifelong link to this man. I had loved him with all my heart but wasn't sure whether I still did. But I also had a career, or what was seemingly becoming less of one. Maybe if I had been given the support by the force I so desperately needed, I would have come to a decision sooner, or would I? When something is slipping away sometimes the only thing you can do is simply what is necessary to survive and get you through another day. There is no logical explanation for it.

The only thing I did know was these two worlds were poles apart and irreconcilable.

I was pretty upset following the meeting. I had an impeccable record, had received numerous awards and a commendation. My staff appraisals were excellent. Yet now, without a shred of evidence, I was untrustworthy. In 'their' opinion.

Peter, back from holiday, suggested we appeal the Confidence Procedure and as such we were brought up in front of the chief constable.

He confirmed the Procedure was in place for a reason and would remain so. If I cut all contact with Dean, then it would end. But he accepted that it was all too raw and, as all communication was monitored, it was not causing too much of a problem, for the time being.

He acknowledged it would be wrong to prevent Dean having contact with his son and added that the force had already prepared a press release, should anything be leaked, which defended my place within the force.

Regarding promotion, with the situation as it was, some posts would not be open to me due to my connections, albeit by circumstance, with an armed crime gang. But all posts would have to be considered on a case by case basis.

I fully accepted his decision.

Meanwhile relations at home with my family were beginning to fracture. My parents and brother could not understand why I simply could not stop contact with Dean and move on with my life. Kent Police had been in touch with them to make statements and my parents had done so, presenting their facts honestly in the form of an evidential statement under oath which could be used at any legal proceedings. They told me they had mentioned the money that Dean had brought with him to France but which they didn't find suspicious at the time, as did none of us. I had no issue with them giving the full facts, I positively encouraged it.

My brother was also required to do the same as he had sold Dean what was now the lookout car.

My brother returned and told me he had stated that Dean owed him the full amount for the Jaguar.

'But he doesn't Andrew, does he, as he's paid you some?'

'Well, he's not paid it all, and if I get any compensation, you can have it. After all, the car is still registered to me.'

'I don't want any money Andrew, what I want is honesty, nothing less will do. This is not some Mickey Mouse show, he is in serious trouble here and I am sick of people lying and twisting stuff, it's not right.'

He looked at me in silence, his eyes narrowed and

cold.

Andrew then attended a second interview with the Kent officers and, on the morning he was due to meet them, I called him around 11am thinking the meeting would be over. I was naturally interested to know how the meeting had gone and was keen to make sure he had clarified the situation with the car payments and what was owed. 'Hey, everything okay? Have you met them yet?'

No, I'm just with them now.'

'Oh okay, I will speak to you later.'

The conversation lasted thirty seconds.

I don't know whether Kent were deliberately trying to fracture my family, to gain some sort of result, but what they dropped into conversation with Peter next, devastated me.

I had to confront it, or rather my brother, for what he had done.

One Sunday I went to my parents where my brother was visiting with his family, eating breakfast in the dining room.

I walked in through the back door and as I approached, I could hear laughter.

Chuckling. It was something that had evaded me for a long time and somehow it felt like my own family was laughing at me. I opened the door and saw the table laid out for breakfast, fit for a king.

King Andrew.

My mouth overruled my thoughts. 'Think it's funny, do you, dropping your own sister in the shit? I knew you were low Andrew, but who would sink that low?' My voice was loud and cut through the sudden silence in the room.

My mum stood up, her face in a state of panic 'Jill, what's the matter, what's happened?'

'Oh, hasn't he told you? He's told Kent Police that I had a go at you for making a statement. He's also told them that, when I rang him that day when he was meeting them, remember Mum, I was here when I made the call...well apparently, I told him not to cooperate with them or make a statement. Now they seem to think I have something to hide?'

My mother's face dropped. 'Andrew? What's this about, what is your sister talking about?'

Silence as he gathered his thoughts, or more appropriately, his excuse, in front of my parents. It seemed like ages before he launched himself from his chair, like a viper striking its prey, and pinned me against the wall. I had tears streaming down my face as he screamed, less than an inch away, his eyes insane and his anger paralysing my body. 'You and your fucking relationships! This is your mess, and nobody else's and quite frankly we are all bored of it. It's time you came to your senses and learned a few lessons, coming in here and telling me, who the fuck do you think you are?!'

'You lied!' I screamed, 'you always lie and don't

care about the consequences for anyone else and it's always been the same. Betraying your own sister, your own blood!'

'Shut your fucking mouth, sooner that bastard is locked away for good the better.'

'Get your hands away now!' I screamed through tears as I struggled to escape, his arms like barriers in the way of my passage.

I could hear Mum crying as I struggled violently to break free. 'Do something,' she yelled at my father, who was standing at the opposite end of the room, just watching events unfold.

But he did nothing. He stood and watched in silence.

I eventually managed to push my brother out of the way and ran as fast as I could through the door of the very place where I should have felt safe.

My family home.

I was distraught and shaking from the shock.

It took a long time for the mental realisation of that incident to sink in, of the strong message that my father's actions, or lack of them, had conveyed.

I ceased contact with them all for some time.

18

Turning the Screws

Autumn 2007 arrived, and Dean Jenkins was sentenced to seventeen years in prison at Maidstone Crown Court for being part of a gang that carried out five armed robberies in the Kent area. I did not go to the Court, I wanted to be kept as far away from it as possible. I certainly didn't want anyone to have the opportunity to work out who I was. The judge summed up the severity of the cases:

'This case involves a series of armed robberies; their execution was ruthless. Each armed robbery falls at the top of the Premier Division. They were planned with military precision. Each armed robbery involved a sawn-off shotgun, the most frightening of weapons of offence. Matters culminated in the New Romney Robbery. Until that occasion you, the armed robbers, had enjoyed rich pickings.

I am satisfied that you Dean Jenkins, on the occasions when two sawn-off shotguns were seen, were the other gunman. You were offering additional support to the ringleader, but you must have appreciated what a dangerous man you were in league with. It has been said that you were in financial problems with your business. You got into substantial debt that is the background for committing these offences. You, Dean Jenkins, are forty years old. It is unusual for a man turning forty to suddenly go on a spree of grave crimes.'

It materialised that Dean had no previous convictions and his business was in debt to the tune of a million pounds and facing collapse. The ringleader had loaned him £18,000 and he was therefore pressured to become involved in the armed robberies to repay the debt.

Analysis of his mobile phone showed him calling me just prior to and following the robberies.

As I read, it dawned. No wonder I had been under suspicion, yet I did not have a clue. I needed to process what I had read. This was a man I no longer recognised.

The Dean I knew was warm, kind, honest and supportive. Proud of the career I had built with total respect for the 'old bill' as he had phrased it. We had plans for our future. I had plans for my career. Life was perfect.

A perfect fantasy.

He alone destroyed it. I had no say. No choice. Out of my control. Dealt another hand, this time of catastrophic proportion. Maybe I was nothing more than an old fool. The man who held my hand one week apparently used the same hand to point a gun to someone's head the next. The man who phoned me with his gentle giant voice overflowing with love had only just stopped screaming in the face of an equally unsuspecting security guard whose head he would apparently not hesitate to blow off. Phoning me before and after robberies, getting his kicks talking to the sergeant and no doubt sharing the joke with the rest of his crew?

Well. Standing ovation, Mr Dean Jenkins. You succeeded in your mission.

You have destroyed me and there is nothing left.

No feelings at all aside from one small issue.

You made me love you.

I sat back, closed my eyes and my mind took up the slack:

Well, fuck you, Dean Jenkins. How dare you put me in this position? How selfish can one person be? Your sentence is fuck all compared to what I'm dealing with. No partner. New baby. Career crumbling before my eyes. Accused of deceit and of being untrustworthy. Fractured family at war. Disowned by friends. Snubbed in the street. Gossiped about. Ridiculed.

But there is nothing I can do to stop any of it. I may as well have carried out the crimes myself. I can't take cover behind those reinforced concrete walls like you can. I can't make a breath without being watched or analysed. Laughed at. Pitied. Destroyed. Total devastation for doing one thing.

Just one simple thing. Again.

Falling in love with you.

And my reward?

You obliterate my whole world.

And I didn't even see it coming.

The sentencing kicked off another course of events. The small matter of the proceeds of crime. Put simply, the police wanted to recoup the stolen money and therefore began to delve into what assets Dean had. Of course, there was very little due to the amount of debt he was in, so it was no surprise when I received another phone call from Kent Police.

'Oh, hi Jill, we noted when we searched your property that you had a new Chrysler Voyager, registration J777GUV parked on the drive. Also, a motorbike in the garage and, obviously, you said the house was in your name.'

'Yes, what of it?'

'Umm well, under the proceeds of crime we need to see proof of ownership.'

I sat down. Shook my head and with a sigh, my voice was tense. 'Are you honestly asking me to prove that I own my stuff when I am not married to him? Are you? He has never lived here; he has a wife and family in Kent, and I am not under investigation. You have no legal right to do this. I have been stripped of everything and here you come with this ridiculous assumption that I would be sat here in a house with a car and bike in the garage, bought with stolen cash? And now I must prove they are not! Who the hell do you think I am?'

'No need to get upset Jill, it's just a question.'

'Just a question. Unbelievable. You will have your proof by the end of the day.'

My life had become a festering boil that never healed. Infection bubbling underneath would rise to the surface and explode, giving temporary relief while the next toxic outburst brewed beneath.

They had their evidence as promised. Everything I owned I had done an honest day's work for. I sensed a small air of disappointment that I was actually able to produce what had been requested.

Chief Constable Grange had retired the same year following an alleged scandal over the misuse of a force credit card and anomalies in his expenses. He was later found to have apparently misused a work computer and a corporate credit card while having an affair. This came to light after the former lover complained to the

Independent Police Complaints Commission, an external police complaints investigating body, two months following the affair.

His departure allowed ACC Edwards to slide across into the still warm driving seat.

One day I found myself sat at my ancient computer, trawling through spreadsheets when the office phone rang.

'Good morning, Sergeant Evans speaking, can I help you?'

'Oh hi, I'm ringing you from the press desk of a National newspaper, I understand you have a child with a convicted armed robber and I'm ringing to...'

My heart felt like it had been shocked and, as her voice tailed away, I felt the four walls closing in on me and a loud buzzing in my ears. I shook my head to regain some composure. 'Sorry, how did you get this direct internal number?'

'We have been looking into the departure of your old Chief Constable Mr Grange, and rang the Police Authority office, who work with the chief officers at headquarters, for comment.

Strangely enough they wouldn't talk but happened to mention your story and where we could get hold of you,' she laughed.

Except it wasn't funny at all.

My mind sprang into action. You are the trade-off. What did you expect?

'Hang on, are you saying they have given you my

details?'

'Well yes, that's why I'm ringing you and, anyway, this story is far better.' She hesitated for a second, 'So, is it true? Were you involved in the armed robberies in Kent?'

I slammed the phone down on its receiver and held it down firmly as if it was an enemy, alive and struggling to be released from its cradle.

This was it; the story was filtering out and it was leaking from the senior ranks. You are a trade-off girl; protect the Senior Management team and we will throw you a sergeant in exchange. This new knife in my back would fit nicely within my collection, joining the one still firmly impaled through my heart, by Dean. I now had a matching pair.

I called Peter on his mobile and tearfully explained what had happened. He was furious but not surprised.

'I'm disgusted. Call Mr Edwards immediately and explain what has happened, you want his guidance right now.'

Late that afternoon I called his mobile phone which seemed to ring for ever before reverting to answer machine. I didn't feel safe leaving a message but within ten minutes he returned my call.

I explained what had happened and asked his advice as to whether I should respond to anything, should it be published, to try and limit what I could only imagine would be sensational headlines.

'It's a matter for you, Sergeant Evans, but I can't imagine anyone would leak anything from our office.'

He did not believe me. 'With respect, sir, how else have they got in touch with me on an internal number? She told me the source was the Authority. I need some help and guidance here, nobody is giving me any instructions and I'm really not strong enough to deal with this, I've only just had my son.' My voice started to break.

'Sergeant Evans, I am glad you made me aware of the situation and I do sympathise, but how you respond is a matter for you, you will just have to weather the storm.'

He didn't want to help me; he wasn't interested. The desert I roamed continued to have little sign of any lifesaving spring.

The press telephone call made me very uneasy. I was suspicious of everything and constantly on edge. As the days passed, thankfully nothing appeared in the news. I thought I would try and get some advice from my Divisional Commander, who had not long been appointed and replaced Superintendent Amphlett. Chief Superintendent Dean Richards was a tall man with a doughy face whose upper body seemed to morph the lower half. He had short wiry hair which was receding and thus created a giant M shape on the front of his head. He seemed friendly enough on initial impression, but I had never worked alongside him so did not have the real makings of him.

I knocked on his door and entered. He sat behind a long desk and in an equally tall black chair. He waved me to take a seat in front of him, the chair being much lower than his desk. I understood this to be a sign of the rank barrier remaining in place. Senior officers often used this tactic so that the person before them was physically positioned lower than them to reinforce the rank structure.

I explained, interspersed by tears, the phone calls to the office and Mr Edwards response. I had not slept since these calls and the weight of worry was now bearing down on me heavily. I found myself welling up even thinking about it.

'Well Jill,' He leaned back in his black chair, hands clasped behind his head, displaying his wet, shirt stained armpits. It was not an attractive sight, hence my vivid memory, 'I personally believe it will be a good thing if it comes out in the press. I'm sure magazines would be interested to run a life article feature, and if I were you, I would speak to them and see if you can get a little money put aside to support you with young Frankie. It would really be no different to the articles you've been asked to write before.'

He was referring to a few articles I had written for *Police Review* magazine about gender and equality within the service. These articles often pulled no punches but explained honestly what really went on behind the scenes, as opposed to what Press Relations chose to release. They had never caused me any internal come backs. Up until this time, I never thought of it in this light.

'If it comes out, we will support you and it will be old news within a few days. I'm sure it will take the weight off your shoulders.'

I left the office feeling a small sense of relief.

A few days later, the *Sun* newspaper reporter contacted me and stated they had been given the story and were going to print. A friendly male voice spoke reassuringly down the telephone. 'I appreciate this is a tough time for you, but we have the story now from a source which makes a spectacular headline and will run it regardless. If you cooperate with me then you can, at least to some extent, control what goes out.'

'Yes, okay, I understand. We have a son, so please can this be played down somewhat with no big feature.'

'Of course.'

And so, I explained the basics; that we had been in a relationship, I didn't have a clue what he was up to but we had simply fallen in love and were planning a life together until this bombshell had hit.

Within days, the newspaper published a double page full size article entitled, 'Cop and Robber.' If that was the played down version, I dreaded to think what the alternative would have been. It couldn't have been much bigger, or more dramatic.

At work the switchboards were inundated with calls from local reporters, magazines and radio shows. The Divisional commander was not in so I called to see the superintendent who assured me not to worry and it would be old news in a short space of time.

As I was leaving his office I was met by the child-like inspector, scuttling along the corridor.

'Jill, how are you feeling? Listen this is going to be a tough time now; do you have any welfare needs?'

Too many to mention, I thought.

'There have been a lot of people calling the station wanting to speak to you to get your story. We can't promise all will be blocked coming through to you in the office, so if they get through, what you say is a matter for you.'

Here we go again. 'It's fine, sir, I understand. It's my problem nobody else's so I will try and deal with it as best I can.'

'Okay. Well, as I said, if you need anything.'

And he was gone.

That same afternoon, just one call came through, a women's magazine. I stood by my decision and corrected a lot of the *Sun* article and tried to protect the police service while simultaneously giving my position. I did not agree, defend or condone what he had done. I had loved him, and I would not prevent him his rights as the father of our son.

They stated they would pay £2000. I didn't really care less. My priority was to correct the circulating stories. The only consolation the money brought was to help me pay off the credit card bill for the Jaguar.

The next day I was summoned to Mr Edwards' office. Peter explained that the purpose of the meeting was to listen to the press release the force intended to make.

'Jill, don't worry now… I've spoken with him today and he's told me that in his opinion, the article in the *Sun* could have been far worse and the force has come out of it quite well, all things considered.'

'I'm just so tired Peter. I can't seem to do right from wrong.'

'I know but listen you have followed their guidance to the letter. Don't worry.'

The meeting that day was a short one. I had very little say in the press release, I simply agreed with it. Interestingly, the force solicitor Samantha Gainard was present in the meeting. Mr Edwards concluded by saying that there would undoubtedly be interest in magazines to run the story and stated if I were to receive any monetary benefit from it, then it could make me liable to disciplinary action.

I couldn't believe what I was hearing. Just the day before, having been told the matter was one for me, I had spoken to a women's magazine. And they were going to pay me. How was this such a coincidence?

Set-up. They are testing to see what you will do; they clearly know about the magazine. Your gut instinct was right not to trust him. You can't trust anyone. Just Peter.

As we left the office, I broke down in tears and Peter ushered me into an empty Conference room

'Come on, it's fine, keep strong now.'

'Peter, they've set me up, nobody wants to help me or give me guidance, they told me speaking to these people was a matter for me, so I've simply tried to control what they print, that's all.'

'Yes, and you have, that *Sun* article could have been far worse.'

'I know, but I've spoken to a women's magazine. They rang me last night and they said they were going to pay me after publication. Edwards has now changed from 'matter for me' to discipline if I receive payment.'

Peter's face dropped. 'Okay, but they haven't paid you or published yet, we can sort this out. Pull the article and that's the end of the problem. It's the money that would be the issue.'

'Let's go back up!' I cried 'I will tell him what's happened. I didn't just now because I feel like I've been handed enough rope to hang myself by them all. He's driving this Peter, and I haven't seen it before.'

'Jill, listen to me now, sit down. You are shaking

and not thinking straight.'

I sat down, head in my hands.

'I agree, something is not right here, it's all too convenient, the timing of all this. Speaking to him won't help.'

'I know', I wailed, but let's just go tell him, I can't take any more, they've broken me down Pete.' I could hear my voice verging on hysterical.

Peter pinched his chin in thought. 'No, we won't go back up, we will get the article pulled and they can keep the payment. The only issue is the payment. You didn't know that yesterday. This is something completely new.'

My mind was like a sinking boat. I was spending what I felt was every minute trying to bail it out to stay afloat. Too much for an unsteady mind to process. Something wasn't right and I was becoming more convinced the goal was to allow me to accomplish my own downfall by my own actions, the very actions I thought were permitted.

That evening I contacted the magazine and explained the developments of the day and that I needed the acceptance to be withdrawn. They refused but agreed to stop any payments.

I didn't sleep again that night. I couldn't trust senior management, so the only thing I could do was continue to be as open as possible. For that reason, on Monday morning, I stood in front of the Divisional Commander Dean Richards, a meeting of my request.

I explained the events of that Friday, the meeting with Edwards and the magazine situation. He shook his head and appeared bemused. 'But you've not received payment?'

'No, sir, I haven't.'

'Then I can't see a problem, you are simply controlling what's already out there, so if they publish, I can't see what the issue is? It's no different to *The Sun*?'

'Sir, I am aware there is a senior management team meeting taking place about me today at 1.30pm. I would be grateful if you could bring what I have told you to their attention. I need advice as I don't know whether I am now bound by the contract. Would they know? If I am and I can't stop the article, then I will try get the article to them before they print it.'

'Yes, of course, and thank you for being so honest. I don't think they will need to see any articles; I will let you know how I get on.'

The following day, late afternoon, he visited my office. 'Jill, as you know I can't divulge what has been said other than I passed the information on that you gave me. All I can say is you need to tread very carefully at present. You also need to be aware of this.' He handed me a piece of paper with the heading, *The Trisha Show*.

'What's this? I've never seen this before?'

'This is an email which has been received via the

Neighbourhood Policing team's website, wanting you on the show. What can you tell me about it?'

I felt something snap. And then it happened. The floodgates burst open; a river of tears mixed with a flow of anger.

'What the hell! Sir, this is nothing to do with me or then again maybe it is another 'matter for me' as you senior officers keep repeating like a stuck record. You've not just had a baby. Just found out your partner has been leading a double life. Lost your career path simply because you have children. The closest you've come to humiliation is the rumour mill circulating about the infidelities of your inspector brother and the dodgy activities he gets up to on his force-issued mobile phone -'

'Sergeant Evans-'

There was no stopping me now. I gulped in more air and raised my voice. 'But oh no! Rank allows that to be conveniently hidden to protect the reputation of the 'Senior Managers'. Police Authority the same; let's use some cannon fodder to deflect from what's happened to the chief constable, oh how generous and convenient for Jill Evans to take one for the boys.'

'Sergeant Evans, calm down.'

'No! I won't calm down, too little too late! What a joke this organisation is.'

'Listen, this *Trisha* email is doing the rounds and I was only trying to forewarn you that one of the

PCSOs has placed some hurtful and inappropriate comments on it.'

'Oh, has she now, and what's being done about that?'

'Umm, she will have some words of advice.'

'Ah great, that'll definitely teach her a lesson, won't it! I stood up. 'I couldn't less care anymore. You lot keep tightening the noose and eventually, I will, no doubt, hang.'

I picked up my stuff and pushed passed him.

I think this was the beginning of my breaking point. It wasn't like me to be so blatantly rude, direct yes, but never disrespectful. My safety mechanisms were all but gone.

The same evening, perfectly timed, the local paper, *The Western Telegraph*, ran a front-page headline: *Local Sergeant had Armed Robber Boyfriend*. A big headline for a small community.

Within one week of the meeting and my outburst, and just under two weeks before Christmas, events took a turn for the worse.

19

Left Outside Alone

I watched as the unmarked cars pulled into the police car park and thought some major operation must be occurring to warrant the arrival of so many. There was a furtive buzz emanating from the senior officer suite before the sound of footsteps echoing louder as they ascended the cream marble stairs.

I was having a cuppa with Gina, the office cleaner, the nicest person you could wish to meet, who had become a good friend. Her concern was genuine, and her company and kindness meant more than she would ever know.

I felt alienated in the station, some colleagues

seemed unsurprisingly distant. They had their own jobs and careers to think about and understood any form of support for me could come with an unwelcome penalty, for example that course you were due on? Well unfortunately, it's been cancelled. That leave you applied for? It can't be granted.

It was simply hassle they could well do without.

A dark shadow appeared in the doorway and a suited figure entered the room. 'Sergeant Evans, could you please accompany me downstairs?'

I felt like I had just been sentenced in court and that the next stop was the cell block.

'Yes, can I ask why?'

'Where you taking her now?' Gina piped up. 'She's only just had that brew.'

'Who are you?' the suited stranger asked.

'Mores the question, who are you in your shiny shoes and suit?' Gina laughed.

'I am an inspector from Discipline and Complaints.'

'Oh, well then, I'm the 'cleaning operative', Gina.' She laughed again.

'Well, then go clean something and keep out of this please.'

I looked at him and narrowed my eyes at his condescending tone, before turning to Gina, nodding that I was okay, and it was fine for her to depart.

She left the office dragging her dirty mop over the front of his black shoes as she looked directly at him. Expressionless. The shoes no longer shone but resembled the aftermath of a slug procession.

Downstairs I was directed into the chief inspector's office where he stood with three other similarly suited males.

The door closed.

'Sit down, Sergeant Evans.'

'What's going on? What's happened? Are my children okay?'

I was starting to panic now. This was quite overwhelming, not to mention intimidating. These men towered over me as I sat below them on another of the smallest strategically arranged chairs.

One of them spoke bluntly.

'As of today, you are officially suspended from police duty. You are not to attend any police establishments, unless invited or accompanied. You will hand over your warrant card and we need to seize your computer and search your locker.'

I took a deep breath and hung my head. Composing myself, I swallowed back the wave of emotion that was building like a tsunami, building from the tips of my toes.

Don't you dare cry, Jill, do not give them the satisfaction. Keep your dignity.

I stood up, reached into my pocket and silently placed my warrant card on the stained coffee ringed desk before me.

'Your computer?'

My pockets aren't that big. 'On my desk.'

'Your locker?'

'I don't have one.'

'Okay, well, I need to remind you that you are not permitted to wear your uniform while under suspension.'

Damn, what will I wear out on Saturday night? Is he serious?

'Do you have anything to say for yourself?'

Four men to suspend me? Am I that dangerous? I looked at them. Expressionless. I felt ice cold. I wasn't even surprised. I sensed for some time they were working against me, leaving me to my own devices, knowing my vulnerabilities and that their lack of guidance would create the opportunities they needed. Enough rope had been issued to hang myself with. Once the chief left and Edwards took the reins, my days were numbered.

My gut feeling had at least, not let me down.

'We will accompany you from the building now, do you have anyone at home for support?'

'I have nobody.'

It was less than two weeks to Christmas, home alone with three children to provide for. They certainly picked their moment.

As I was marched along the corridor to the exit, I looked up and saw Gina standing at the top of the stairs leaning on her mop.

'Oi! Where are you taking her?'

But they didn't respond.

'Bloody jobsworths,' she muttered as her voice faded into the distance.

We reached the door and, as I exited, I heard the lock turn behind me.

The screw turned tighter.

I could sense eyes peering from every window overlooking the yard, which was eerily quiet, as if everyone knew what was happening and scuttled behind doors until it was done.

I felt humiliated.

Seventeen years of service has come to this. Where was I to go from there? I felt like the sand in an egg timer. Slowly, grain by grain, my world fell through the hole, regardless of my actions to try and plug it.

Don't you cry yet, you hear me? Jill! Come on! Hold it together, keep your head up. Nobody has seen you cry like this and you aren't about to start now. Not for them. That's what they want. To break you. Well, they won't break you. Not you.

Driving home the radio played random jolly Christmas songs and my blank face remained in place, as if I was wearing a clay mask I did not want to crack. I opened my front door and the house was silent and still. I walked over to the fire in the lounge to warm myself as I was shaking, but it wasn't from cold. It was rage.

The Christmas tree looks so pretty; you have done such a good job of that, Jill.

By the way, it's okay, you can cry now.

I sank down to my knees and the floodgates opened. The mask cracked and dissolved with the tears.

When I had gathered myself together, my first call was to Peter, who had not been given any forewarning of my suspension. As my representative, normal practice would have been to give him a heads-up so he could be on hand to provide emotional support in the aftermath of such a monumental development. This had been inadvertently 'overlooked'.

Within a week, I was back on the front page of the local newspaper, the details clearly leaked with an official one-liner from Professional Standards confirming my suspension.

20

Happy Pills and Shopping Lists

Dean. 'Hey, Gorgeous, how has your day been?' His voice on the phone was so distinctive.

'Hmm, well not that great, I've been suspended.'

My voice was muted.

'What? What does that mean? Can you still bring Frankie to see me?'

'I'm sorry Dean, I won't be coming any time soon. It's done. I have too much to deal with down here and I need to focus on that. I am now suspended. I know they are looking for any way to get rid of me, so I need to stop the contact.'

'But he is my son, I have rights.'

You have rights!? I took a deep breath and my voice launched straight to anger mode. 'Ah yes, you do don't you, to hell with me and my tormented world. Maybe I should take a leaf out of your selfish book and, in fact, every other man I've ever intimately trusted and instead, look after number one!' I continued, on a roll. 'I am sick of hearing of everyone else's woes. You brought this upon us and I'm out here trying to keep my head above water, while you sit there reminding me of your bloody rights? Selfish is the word. Well, right now I own the fucking rights. It's done. It's over. I cannot deal with anyone else's issues bar my own and the kids'. So, your rights can join you on vacation while I try and keep what is left of my world together.'

I replaced the receiver with a bang.

I didn't feel as I should have felt ending a relationship. There were no tears and I wondered whether I was capable of feeling any emotion ever again. I just couldn't seem to find anything in the wilderness of my soul except a small burning ember of strength which solely kept me alive. It continued to burn, despite everything, even though the thick black choking smog of endless doom tried desperately to smother it.

A few days before Christmas, Peter visited. I was in bits, humiliated by my suspension and back to the safety of my pyjamas and the sofa. My suspicions were in stealth mode; any callers to the house found me crawling on the floor below window level to check them out from the safety of a small window overlooking the porch. I wouldn't dare open the door before I knew who was there.

It had become a huge priority to try and stop the magazine from publishing the article. Peter called them from my lounge on speakerphone.

'We are so sorry Mr Dickenson; we have been trying to get hold of Jill at the station and headquarters, but they told us we were not to have any communication with her due to the terms of her suspension.'

'Okay,' replied Peter, 'did they ask to see the article?'

'No, they didn't.'

'Okay, and it's definitely running?'

'Yes, it will be in the New Year edition.'

'Okay, but no payments are to be made. Do you understand?'

'Yes, fully. No payments.'

Happy New Year to me.

In the run up to New Year a neighbour knocked at the door and told me she had been having strange phone calls to the house, asking questions about what she knew of me as a neighbour. The following day I returned home and noticed a car I did not recognise parked opposite my house. I quickly went inside but within seconds there was a knock. I opened the door.

'Jill Evans?'

I just looked at the woman standing before me.

Petite, slim, friendly.

Definitely not police.

'I'm a reporter from the *Wales on Sunday* newspaper.'

I groaned in despair. 'I'm sorry but the terms of my suspension prevent me from speaking to you.'

'I understand that, but I think it's important we get your story across. I kind of get the feeling that what has been put out at present deliberately puts you in a bad light.'

'Can I ask, would your contact happen to be from somewhere within Dyfed Powys Police headquarters by any chance?'

Her cheeks coloured and her eyes momentarily dropped to the floor.

'Umm, I can't tell you that, but there is renewed interest in your case due to the police backtracking in their advice and suspending you.'

'As I said, I can't speak to you.'

I closed the door and she shouted, nose up against the glass, 'It's okay, I will speak to other sources you know.'

I sighed. More newspaper articles.

I picked up the phone and updated Professional Standards.

The following Sunday, I decided to escape with the children to Swansea, to get out and away from the noise of my situation. As I filled up the car with fuel on a Swansea garage forecourt I walked inside to pay and my attention was drawn to the newspaper stand.

The front page of the *Wales on Sunday* had a large picture of someone in police uniform, someone who looked very much like me: *Hero Sarge Suspended. New probe into decorated cop over jailed lover.*

That looks like me. Shit. It is me!

I picked up a copy and covered the remaining copies with other newspapers in the ridiculous hope that nobody would see them.

I hadn't seen the picture before and I racked my brains as to when and where it was taken. Then it dawned. It was taken at a local show by, I'm sure, a police photographer. I never had a copy of the picture, so it took little detective work to surmise where the leak continued to drip from. There was no escape from the pressure.

I had little contact with the police since being suspended. Genuine welfare was non-existent, what little they did was simply to tick a box for compliance. There was no serious intention of support and certainly no understanding of what I was going through.

I was appointed a welfare officer; the same male inspector who had previously advised me that my standards were too high. Oddly enough, I believe he was a relative of Chief Superintendent Richards, but he was not *my* supervisory inspector. He called me one afternoon on my mobile. I had not been answering calls from unknown numbers and was back to being extremely cautious regarding all outside contact.

'Hi, is that Jill?'

'Yes.'

'Blimey, you are a hard girl to get hold of. It's a good job we are not having an affair. I would never see or hear from you!' He laughed. There was an awkward silence. His misplaced humour was insulting.

'Sir, what do you want?'

'I need to visit, tick the box regarding welfare. You know how it goes. Can I come around in the next hour?'

'Fine'.

The visit was uncomfortable. I remained in my pyjamas and when the doorbell rang, I had forgotten I was expecting him and did my usual crawl by reconnaissance to the window.

My hair was dishevelled, no trace of makeup as I opened the door and ushered him inside.

'How are you feeling, you look fine? He spoke with arrogance. My thoughts leaped into action. Oh, yes, of course I'm fine.

'I don't know, sir, how does it look like I feel?'

'Ah not too bad, perhaps you need to get yourself down to the doctor and get some happy pills in you.'

Really.

'Thing is, you need to look on the bright side. If I were you, I would go for the silver lining. If there is not a movie in this story, there is definitely a book.'

Every senior officer seemed to be sent to encourage me to do the very thing that would apparently cost me my job. Get rid of him, I thought, you don't need this.

I was beginning to feel like the only trustworthy conversations to be had were either with my own mind or with Peter. I could quite easily identify how easy it was to dupe people who were vulnerable and make them feel safe in doing the very thing that would ultimately provide ammunition for their downfall. It was devious and cowardly.

'Do you know what, sir, with respect, I don't need these visits. You can leave.'

'Oh, come on now, cheer up. Things will get better soon.'

'I want you to leave.' My tone was cold.

I stood up and accompanied him to the door, locking it behind him, just as they had done to me.

I explained what had happened to Peter, and he suggested some emotional help with the force councillor. It took some time to build up enough courage to trust this process and eventually several sessions were booked. I spent a lot of time crying throughout, but somehow talking to a stranger genuinely seemed to help.

Until one morning.

'Jill, before we start, I'm obliged to let you know that, unusually, having done a few sessions with you, I have received direct requests from Chief

Superintendent Mel Evans asking me to detail what we have discussed. Obviously due to confidentiality, I need to run this by you.'

I looked at her, open-mouthed. The trust I had built up with her evaporated in those few seconds.

'I'm sorry. What? Is that normal practice?'

'No, it's not. He has made the approach as he wishes to know what you are discussing with me and he has been most persistent, I'm afraid. It's up to you how I respond.'

'I don't consent to him knowing anything, and I really don't think there is any point in these sessions anymore.'

It seemed I had no privacy for my feelings, I couldn't even vent them to my councillor without the wolves at the door baying for my blood.

I had nothing to hide, it just seemed like Professional Standards felt they owned the rights to everything concerning me, including my soul. The pressure was mounting. I seemed to take two steps forward before three steps back and it was destroying me.

I stopped the sessions and withdrew to the safety of my home.

Before the week was out, the magazine article was published. It was nothing like I understood it to be. There were pictures of me in uniform I didn't even know existed and it was written along the lines of me professing my undying love for Dean, and that I would stand by him. It was a far cry from what I had originally told them.

Peter contacted them to complain as we had kept a very early proof regarding what had been agreed and it was nothing like what was on the page before us.

We received an email response. *We had written to Ms Evans at the police station but received no response. The force told us we were unable to contact her and so the final article was run, without her approval. We are sorry for any distress this may have caused.*

The force could have looked at the article prior to it going to press but they chose not to, and I believe this was deliberate. The worse the article was, the better. More ammunition for them to fire and assist the formulation of their charges.

'Sorry' didn't really cut it.

Following this, Kent Police released their written findings to me, having verbally done so to the force at a much earlier stage.

It would appear that Jill Evans and her family have been completely duped by Jenkins. There is nothing to indicate that any of the family had any knowledge of any criminal activity by him in the months leading up to his arrest.

My suspension, however, remained in force.

The weeks and days that followed were largely taken up by my attending legal meetings with Peter and my allocated federation barrister. The process was not a smooth one.

I was formally charged with misconduct offences, despite the fact that there was no change in circumstances from when I was put under the Confidence Procedure, the policy document for which clearly stated: *It must be emphasised that these procedures will only be invoked when criminal prosecution or misconduct procedures are not possible.*

What had been non-misconduct under the Confidence Procedure, had now suddenly become misconduct. Peter questioned this and asked for clarification, but the response was unhelpful: It was simply the way it was.

My charges spanned two A4 pages:

Honesty and Integrity and General Conduct
Being a police sergeant with Dyfed Powys Police, you have failed to act with honesty or integrity concerning your relationship with Dean Jenkins and matters arising out of that relationship, in that you:

1) Formed a relationship with Jenkins.

2) During the subsistence of this relationship you knew or ought reasonably to have known that Jenkins was someone with whom police officers should not associate, socially or at all.

3) On 20th March 2006 Jenkins, in company with others, committed the first of a series of 5 armed robberies in Kent.

4) In July 2006 you became pregnant with Jenkins' child.

5) On the 31st October 2006 Jenkins and others committed the fifth armed robbery in the course of which one robber was shot dead by police (after he had shot at police officers) and Jenkins was arrested.

6) Jenkins was charged with committing the armed robberies and remanded into custody where he has remained ever since. Despite this, you maintained a relationship with him.

7) You failed to cooperate with and /or obstructed the Kent Police investigation into the armed robberies.

8) On the 2nd November 2007 Jenkins was sentenced to 17 years in prison for 5 armed robberies despite this, you maintained a relationship with him.

9) You have inappropriately engaged with the media in relation to your relationship with Jenkins.

10) You have manipulated and misled senior supervisory officers in relation to your relationship with Jenkins and your associated involvement with the media.

11) You knew or ought to have known the above behaviour would bring discredit upon the police service.

I was sent initial disclosure in preparation for my hearing. This consisted of statements taken by Professional Standards from literally most people who had ever had contact with me. There were sheets of questionnaires where people were asked directed questions about what they knew of my relationship with Dean, or of the newspaper articles. It did not take a genius to see that they were dredging the barrel to make a case against me, in particular the charge of bringing the force into disrepute. They were asking leading questions about 'public' comment or observations on the matter. Ironically one such statement was from the PCSO who had circulated the *Trisha* email with her own inappropriate comments: *Several members of the public spoke to me about this matter saying how can she get away with this, being related to a bank robber.*

I doubted very much this was from the public, it was certainly unnecessary and malicious, but more likely her opinion. This sort of weak, unevidenced comment was the strength of their case. It was in the minority compared to many more statements they had gathered from, for example, regular officers who worked with me on my team: *Most people have laughed about the articles. Jill has said it was nothing to do with her and that is the general belief. She is an excellent sergeant and let's face it, it was bound to come out some time due to the nature of the story. There are a lot of jealous people looking to stick the boot into that girl, not really fair, as she brought none of it upon herself.*

I was also served with a large file of photographs, which initially confused me.

I opened the file and saw it contained sixty-four A4 blown-up prints of all the photographs on my phone.

Photos of me semi-clad state showing my expanding pregnancy and intimate photos of me in a state of undress. Photos of my children. Everyday private photos that you would take on your phone, but the more intimate ones were clearly meant for Dean's eyes only. As I looked closely, my mouth open, I realised these were the very same photographs Kent had assured me had only been viewed and eliminated from the criminal aspect of the enquiry and had not been passed to Professional Standards.

They had lied.

I felt sick.

My children. My semi-clad naked body. Extremely personal photographs.

I was devastated.

This disclosure meant these pictures would be in full circulation at the hearing. The prosecution, defence, the panel, the admin teams at Kent and Dyfed Powys and whoever else got their hands on them. Eventually the whole of my force, maybe even the papers the rate the leaks were springing. The humiliation was mounting.

Peter immediately lodged a complaint and asked for the photos to be withdrawn.

I had now been appointed an investigating officer.

He was arrogant, self-assured and again, seemed to relish every part of his difficult job. He had a large oval head which reminded me of the game I had a child, Mr Potato Head. Except his rather large ears could not, unlike my game, be mixed or matched.

He responded stating they would not be removed, the photographs not his ears, and to argue it at the pending disciplinary hearing.

My humiliation quickly shifted to anger. How dare they include my children; this was nothing to do with them. I wouldn't let them dissect every part of my life as if it was their God given right. Enough was enough.

I had no issue with my phones being checked but did not consent for my photos to be circulated. I felt that both Kent and Dyfed Powys had acted unlawfully with my personal data with the sole purpose to humiliate me.

Dyfed Powys then produced another blinding justification for the presence of the photographs: *The photographs are required as they are key evidence to prove that Jill Evans was in an intimate relationship with Dean Jenkins. They will remain as part of the disclosure. We have acted appropriately.*

Key evidence. I think my pregnancy was the biggest clue of my intimate relationship with Dean Jenkins, along with the fact that it was the reason I was in this position in the first place.

I had brought the relationship to their attention. Up until that point I was blissfully unaware I was in a relationship with an armed robber.

The explanation was ludicrous, a comedy, and simply proved there was no other goal than total humiliation for me as an officer, a woman and a mother.

I had no choice but to let the situation run, as to argue the case was piling on more stress and was like banging my head against a brick wall.

I lodged an external, formal complaint against both forces for breaching my right to privacy.

Time ticked on and I was heading into the two-year anniversary since this whole sorry situation had arisen. The not knowing was torturous, and any requests for timeline updates were ignored.

It wasn't long before they fired their next round.

Peter had stood by me one million percent. He had spoken up when things were wrong or when practice was unethical. He had kept abreast of the fluid movement of the investigation at times when I was unable to understand or function. And, most importantly, he had always been there for me, keeping a watch over my welfare. He was like my right arm and I seriously don't think I would have survived without him and his genuine kindness.

He came to visit, flushed in the face and clearly furious.

'Oh, God no, what's happened now Pete?'

'This is classic, they want me to provide a witness statement regarding the meetings we have attended with various parties, the facts of which are not under dispute.'

I dropped my head. I knew this meant that once he

gave a statement, he could no longer represent me as a federation friend.

So, there it was. The missile had struck my last rock of support.

'Well, I am not doing it; I am quite within my rights to decline and this is absolutely disgusting. I know their game,' he said.

'Peter, if you need to do it, I totally understand as they will probably try stitch you up some other way if you don't. Please, don't feel bad.'

'No, you don't understand, I am not doing it! I am with you to the end; this situation is so unfair, and I am not obliged to legally comply with what they are asking. I have already emailed them my response.'

It didn't take long for a reply to Peter's email to come flying back from the investigating Inspector :

I have considerable reservations over your decision, which I feel I ought to bring to your attention. Put shortly, I am very concerned that you will find yourself potentially in a conflict of interest between your duties as a police officer and your duties as Sergeant Evans' friend which may place you in a very difficult professional situation. It would be unfortunate if misconduct proceedings move forward against Sergeant Evans and you find yourself a potential witness in those proceedings. I recognise that it is a matter for you to determine if there is a conflict of interest in acting as a friend, but consider that you should be made aware of the interactions where you are considered to be a potential witness. I therefore ask you to re consider your refusal to provide a witness statement.

An email sent under the guise of genuine concern but with one sole purpose; to extinguish my defences and allies.

Peter stuck to his guns for as long as he possibly could. To him veiled threats were like water off a duck's back. The date of the hearing was set, almost two years to the date of that fateful Halloween night way back in 2006.

21

Stop – Rewind – Play

I sat and watched my reflection in the mirror. Hair wet, limp, almost mimicking the current state of my body. My mind patched together with imaginary fraying plasters. I took in the frail image.

I had never been pushed beyond my combined limits before. Physical limits are one thing but when mind and body has been tested for such a sustained amount of time, there has to be some inevitable fall out. I could see it in my reflection. My face was drawn, and my eyes had lost the life and spark that had once burned within them. Old man time had also taken his toll and they were dull, lifeless and sad. My forehead resembled a ploughed and furrowed field, but there was no prospect of new growth or life. Simply long old corridors that led back to the festering tombs within my mind.

Stress had become my normal.

In my peripheral vison, I could see the silhouette of a grey suit. Waiting.

I switched on the hair dryer and took comfort from the warm air on my face.

The suit could wait.

My fate once again was in the hands of someone else.

Make up on. Hair ready. I looked at the suit.

It's time.

Moments later I looked at my full reflection as the suit came to life on my pale limbs.

I took a deep breath in.

Showtime.

As I arrived at police headquarters I walked slowly down the drive to the main public entrance.

There was a line of six marked police vehicles parked up outside, and I could feel twelve pairs of eyes watching my very step.

Click. Click. Click. My heels were almost comforting, my only company on that walk of shame.

The eyes watched.

Raise your head. You have nothing to be ashamed of. You are better than this.

I looked up and my welling eyes locked with the

driver of the first vehicle.

40.

He smiled, uncomfortably, but didn't move. I didn't need sympathy. I needed strength.

The ember still glowed within me and, like Superman needs Kryptonite, it was all that kept me alive.

I shut my eyes and felt a tear roll down my cheek.

My legal team was waiting.

At the eleventh-hour Peter had made a statement and handed the federation's Friend role to another from South Wales Police. It was a conscious choice by us both, as we had no trust for anyone within our own force.

His statement could be used in my defence, to validate my presentation of facts, but he couldn't sit with me for support in the hearing.

The room was set. The long tables at the front would seat the presiding officers who looked over a horseshoe arrangement with prosecution and defence teams on either side. Witnesses required to give their evidence sat directly in front of the panel.

In a police misconduct hearing, there is no requirement, as in a court of law, for people to swear an oath to tell the truth, however that is the expected standard. Equally, there is no necessity to prove cases against the subject beyond all reasonable doubt. It is simply based on the balance of probabilities.

I watched as the panel filed in. An assistant chief constable and two superintendents from external police forces. This was not the original panel.

Professional Standards made last-minute changes to the presiding officer. My team raised a complaint and questioned this action, but it was simply dismissed.

I watched the female superintendent and wondered whether she would perhaps place a little female rationale on my situation. My hope quickly dissolved.

'We will have these in the interval,' she announced to her excited male colleagues, as she placed a box of Welsh cakes on the desk. 'I was up late making them especially for you.'

I cringed for a moment and sighed, so ridiculous was the scene. This wasn't some movie premiere where snacks were required. This was my life in the balance.

My future.

My barrister commenced with an objection to the inclusion of the photographs in the hearing bundle. The panel consulted with the prosecution team, rejected his request and insisted the inclusion was perfectly legitimate.

My heart sank. More humiliation afoot.

The first witness was acting Chief Constable Andy

Edwards and upon being questioned by the prosecution, my barrister took to the podium. As the questioning got under way, my mind resembled an ant's nest that had just been doused in hot water, my thoughts racing erratically and fuelled with frustration and anger.

B: 'Can we look at the Service Confidence Procedure. It's right, isn't it, that the reason this occurred was because it was felt that criminal and misconduct procedures were not appropriate?'

E: 'Yes.'

B: 'You were made aware during the course of that meeting that the Kent investigation team had concluded in their report that Jill Evans had been completely duped?'

E: 'No.'

B: 'Professional Standards neglected to tell you that?'

E: 'I was only aware Kent Police suggested Jill's response was hostile and uncooperative but that was not in keeping with Jill's version.'

So, Kent Police cleared me of any wrongdoing, yet my own force were not informed? Or were they, and you simply chose to overlook that important piece of information, being so hell-bent to find something to charge me with?

B: 'You were well aware that there was ongoing

contact between Sergeant Evans and Jenkins by visits and telephone, yes?'

E; 'Yes.'

B: 'You were asked your view at this meeting whether there was evidence of criminal misconduct matters, and you said it was marginal in relation to allegations of a lack of cooperation. Chief Superintendent Amphlett then stated a form of discipline would seem inappropriate at this stage, bearing in mind Jill was not being treated as a suspect, then goes on to say in the minutes and is agreed by all present, that any misconduct response should have been initiated previously. Indeed, Mr Amphlett had at that time been made aware by Kent of the concerns held regarding her cooperation and yet this wasn't considered a misconduct matter?'

E: 'No.'

B: 'In fact there are no further investigations from Kent involving Jill after this Service Confidence meeting?'

E: 'No.'

B: 'The then chief constable, Mr Grange's, statement reads; *Permission was being sought for Sergeant Evans to visit Jenkins in prison, and the consensus was formed that she should be allowed to conduct a visit. The Service conduct issues were solely about her ties and continued contact with Jenkins.* The report goes on to say it was agreed there were no Confidence issues but it was recognised that there would be a need for contact with Jenkins due to the child involved.'

E: 'Yes.'

B; 'And nothing's changed there?'

E: 'No.'

B: 'So there is confirmation of no criminal charges, involvement and no misconduct offences in her visiting and her contact with Jenkins. Also, her alleged lack of cooperation was not considered as misconduct. If it was, charges should have been instigated previously. All this was conveyed in the notice she was served?'

Yet my charges include allegations that predate this time. How could that be?

E: 'Yes, at that stage, based on the information we had that day.'

B: 'But it doesn't say that does it, not what Sergeant Evans was told. It says Service Confidence procedure is for situations where it is considered that the use of criminal or misconduct processes are inappropriate due to the circumstances involved.'

E; 'Yes, up to that point.'

B: 'Does it say *up to that point?*'

E: 'No.'

B: 'The notice then says the force disapproves of your association with Mr Jenkins, his immediate family and co-accused. What it doesn't say is that contact, telephone contact or visiting was not compatible with being a police officer. It doesn't say that does it?'

E: 'No, she had been advised she could contact Jenkins in respect of welfare issues and the panel agreed in August 2007 these were still ongoing.'

B: 'So that didn't mean she was to cease all contact did it?'

E: 'No.'

B: 'Yet this is one of her charges? Hmm.'

Hmm exactly. One of my charges was for having continued contact with Dean. Contact they authorised.

B: 'A statement makes a person liable to prosecution if anything stated within is false. So, according to yours, who was present at the time of this meeting?'

E: 'Superintendent Mel Evans, Professional Standards and Sergeant Evans.'

B: 'In your statement you refer to Peter Dickenson as being present?'

E: 'Umm, well no that was my mistake. If she had wanted him there, she could have had. Superintendent Evans made the arrangements, I must have made a mistake.'

How convenient.

B: 'A mistake. Really. Now the Service Confidence panel meeting wasn't your first involvement with the matter, was it?'

E: 'It was my first engagement with the matter.'

B: 'It wasn't your first involvement with the matter was it, sir?'

E: 'I can only refer to my previous answer.'

B: 'Your witness statement was made before Mr Grange and Mr Taylor, the deputy chief, made theirs?'

E: 'Right.'

B: 'You state; *I was aware that Ps Evans had been in contact with the chief constable prior to this meeting, although I was not party to any discussions about her.* That was misleading, wasn't it, as you *were* party to discussions that had taken place prior to this date concerning Sergeant Evans and Dean Jenkins?'

E: 'My only engagement was regarding some welfare issues with her. I was just a sounding board but didn't have authority for those areas.'

B: 'Your statement; *I was not party to any discussions that had taken place, and this was my first involvement with the matter.* Inaccurate to say the least. In fact, your first involvement was in November 2006 when you spoke to Peter Dickenson, shortly after Jenkins arrest!'

E: 'Can I ask when that took place? Was it a meeting? Were minutes taken?'

B: 'Peter Dickenson statement, *I spoke to ACC*

Edwards and sought his view on Jill's consideration for seeing Dean. Mr Edwards was not very supportive and indicated the relationship should end.

E: 'He asked my view in what capacity? I cannot recollect that conversation but if it did take place all I can say was it was something instigated by Peter Dickenson, possibly in the corridor, possibly over a cup of tea, along the lines have you heard about Jill? I wasn't acting in any capacity. Could I ask what Mr Dickenson says then?'

B: 'And in fact after speaking to Mr Dickenson, you went and spoke to Mr Taylor about the same issue? Statement of Mr Taylor; *Early in her pregnancy I recall having a discussion with ACC Edwards who had received a query in relation to her contact with Dean Jenkins. Mr Edwards and I considered that she should be allowed to visit Dean Jenkins so she could make informed decisions about her future. Chief Constable Grange was briefed with our views.*

E: 'I can only recollect a number of comments about the position she found herself in.'

B: 'And he goes on; *I did not personally convey any decision to Ps Evans, this was done by ACC Edwards who received the initial enquiry.*

E: 'I will come back to my previous point, there were welfare issues.'

B: 'I agree with you, but what I'm asking is whether this happened?'

E: 'I can't recollect the details.'

B: 'But you spoke to Mr Grange about Jill's welfare

issues?'

E: 'Yes there was a discussion.'

B: 'Okay, so I bring you back to your statement. Where you say you were not party to any discussions in relation to this matter and the Service Confidence meeting was your first involvement...it clearly wasn't and that is not accurate.'

You are making yourself look ridiculous.
Silence.

B: 'Now in November 2007 you spoke to Jill directly on the phone?'

E: 'Yes.'

B: 'She wanted advice about speaking to the press?'

E: 'Yes.'

B: 'Did you tell her it was a matter for her?'

E: 'Yes.'

B: 'Did you say she shouldn't cooperate with the press?'

E: 'No.'

B: 'Another one of her charges. Hmm. Now there was much press interest in Dyfed Powys at the time. Something of a storm?'

E: 'Yes.'

B: 'And there were a number of leaks in relation to all sorts of matters?'

E: 'I wouldn't go so far to say there were leaks.'

B: '*Western Mail* article 2007. *An insider in the Force*

said she'd been moved to a different role since she told senior officers of her lover's criminal history. Who was that?'

E: 'No idea.'

B: 'So, again, would you accept from October onwards there were a number of unauthorised releases?'

For God's sake, what is the matter with you? It's like pulling teeth.

E: 'I think it would be naive to expect the media wouldn't try and get information from any source available.'

B: 'The end of November *The Sun* published an article about Sergeant Evans. You saw it that morning while chairing a Corporate Strategy Board meeting in Llanelli. Also present were senior police officers, including Chiefs Superintendents Richards, Amphlett and Evans, civilians and other external agencies. Also Peter Dickenson'

E: 'Yes.'

B: 'Do you remember the newspaper being left open on that page outside the meeting room, seemingly for people to look at on their way in?'

E: 'I don't.'

B: 'When you came into the meeting you opened it with a light hearted reference to reading *The Sun*. Do you remember that?'

E: 'I wouldn't have made a light hearted reference.'

B: 'And people in the room laughed about it.'

E: 'No.'

B: 'Mr Dickenson's statement reads; *Mr Edwards opened the meeting with a light-hearted quip in respect of the meeting being delayed because he had been reading* The Sun *newspaper. The comment was greeted with laughter around the table. I considered the comment to be inappropriate and unprofessional, especially as made in the presence of invited guests.*

E: 'No.'

B: 'And again in your statement; *The article caused me great concern.*

E: 'Yes.'

B: 'Can I play this to you? I'm playing a cd and I will ask the officer to assist me with it.'

Edwards suddenly shuffled in his seat and looked like a rabbit caught in headlights.

The cd is played, audio of Edwards voice; *Good morning everybody, sorry about the delay, I was reading* The Sun *newspaper and I'm afraid I got side-tracked as it were.' Laughter in room.*

B: 'That was you at the beginning of the meeting?'

E: 'Umm...well.'

B: 'Was it or wasn't it?'

E: 'Umm.'

B: 'Well?'

E: 'It certainly sounded like me.

B: 'I can play more if you like?'

E: 'No I'm happy to accept that's what it was.'

I watched, animated, as the Chair of the panel cut in sharply

Chair: 'Can I ask for what purpose the recording was made and who recorded it?'

Mel Evans rose quickly and scuttled out of the room, as if in a panic.

A spanner in the works. Truth costs nothing, lies can cost you everything.

B: 'It was a recording of the meeting; it wasn't just the comment on its own. You are welcome to listen to the rest to confirm if you like?'

Chair: 'Ugh, no, no, it's alright.'

E: 'I want to question the origin of that tape. Was it a formal recording of the meeting?'

B: 'It is. So. As I said before, it was a light-hearted reference to the article and people laughed. Do you accept that, now?'

E: 'It was patently obvious to me that everyone was aware of *The Sun* newspaper.'

He was on the back foot, his voice agitated and

somehow protesting far too much.

E: 'I had *only* been acting deputy Chief for a matter of weeks when I had to stand in for the chief within an hour of him suddenly leaving office after being spoken to by the Police Authority. I had to deal with a storm of media interest. I liaised with every assembly member, MP, staff members within the force, community, national and local media. Her Majesty's Inspectorate and all the sensitive committees Mr Grange dealt with. Every move I made was looked upon.'

My thoughts digested his words.

I really don't care Mr Edwards. You are paid a huge amount of money for the rank you hold, and problems are part of the territory. And yet here you sit, with the woe is me act. You have no excuses. I contrarily was not paid to be duped, investigated and hounded out of my career while managing my pregnancy and an emotional breakdown. Your excuses, *you*, are pitiful.

He continued to protest;

E: 'If I was seen to be folding it would impact on the Organisation. I had to display my leadership. I outlined I had been reading *The Sun*, that was a fact. If I had held my head in my hands and shown my true feelings it would have sent a negative effect to the senior officers around the table. I did not think lightly of it but I wasn't going to share that with everyone.'

B: 'So, you hadn't dealt with anything like the media storm you found yourself in?'

E: 'It was the most challenging period of my career.'

B: 'Similar to Sergeant Evans. Yet despite being an experienced officer you had nothing to draw on?'

E: 'I had plenty of experience in my banks thank you!'

Plenty of excuses you mean.

B: 'Hmm, so do you now accept you made a light-hearted reference to the *Sun* article?'

E: 'I was explaining I was late.'

B: 'But people laughed. Do you think that to be professional from a man in your position, Acting Chief Constable?'

E: 'I didn't milk it if that's what you are suggesting.'

B: 'People laughed Mr Edwards!'

E: 'I heard a few people laugh.'

B 'And you didn't find that surprising?'

E: 'Well people make their own judgement.'

B: 'You had spoken to Mr Dickenson ahead of the meeting on the way in?'

E: 'I might well have done.'

For goodness sake.

B: Again, Mr Dickenson's statement; *I spoke with ACC Edwards in the entrance to the hotel. He had read the Sun article and said he was not worried about it as it could have been a lot worse and the Force had come out of it quite well. He anticipated further media interest and invited Jill and I to his office that day at 3pm to prepare a press release.*

E: 'I can't recollect the exact discussion. It could have been worse. Yes.'

B: 'A lot worse you said.'

E: 'It was certainly bad enough!'

B: 'You said the Force had come out of it quite well.'

E: 'I don't recollect that comment.'

Hmm, of course you don't.

B: 'Later that afternoon you had a meeting with Sergeant Evans, Mr Dickenson and Samantha Gainard, the Force solicitor.'

E: 'Yes.'

B: 'And in that meeting Sergeant Evans told you she had spoken to *The Sun*.'

E: 'Yes, it says in my statement Sergeant Evans stated that while she had spoken to *The Sun* newspaper she had not engaged with them.

B: 'Now pause there, is *engaged* a word *she* actually used or was that a word you would use, as we have heard it often throughout your evidence.'

E: 'No that would be a word I'd use.'

B: 'Sergeant Evans didn't actually say the word *engaged*?'

E: 'No.'

At last.

B: 'So she made it clear to you she had spoken to them but not everything in that article had come from her.'

E: 'Yes, that was certainly what she was saying.'

B: 'If we look at the article, one quote is from Sergeant Evans and then later they refer to a *friend* relating to them what Sergeant Evans had said.'

E: 'Yes.'

B: 'So that's what she told you in the meeting?'

E: 'She said she hadn't engaged; the quotes could have been from any number of people who would have heard her saying that sort of thing.'

B: 'But you've said *engage* was definitely not her word, it was yours?'

E: 'Yes.'

B: 'You went on to talk about future press interest that would inevitably follow. You told her if she was to cooperate with any magazines *and* receive payment, she may be looking at misconduct issues?'

E: 'Well there were two issues. I felt that dealing with the media could potentially lead to misconduct.'

B: 'Yet you didn't tell her this, you said it was a matter for her, she has never been told *not* to speak to the press?'

E: 'No, I felt that payment would be the aggravating factor.'

B: 'And you also reiterated it was a matter for her if she responded to the press but if she received payment it would amount to misconduct. You also say in your statement that you specifically asked Sergeant Evans at the end of the meeting whether there was anything else you should be made aware of. You never asked that did you?'

E: 'I did.'

B: 'Is that something you have added in hindsight Mr Edwards, to fit one of her later charges and because of what later transpired with the publication of the magazine article?'

Of course it is, as one of my charges is that I have misled and manipulated senior officers, so, by you saying you asked me a question, which you didn't, I have apparently manipulated you. Really. A female sergeant manipulating an acting chief constable. Maybe the experience in your banks is not as great as you think it is.

E: 'No, no certainly not!'

B: 'Okay, thankyou Mr Edwards, I will pick this up with the next witness.'

R: 'Panel, the next witness is Samantha Gainard, the Force solicitor who took the minutes of the meeting we have just been referring to. Before then I suggest, with your permission, a short break?'

Panel: 'Agreed, fifteen minutes please.'

I got up from my seat and went to the restroom where I splashed cold water on my face. Leaning on the sink I looked at myself in the mirror, as if having a conversation with my reflection.

A senior officer caught out, yet the panel question the integrity of our evidence, as if horrified we have obtained it? This panel has without doubt been handpicked to deliver the required results. That is why it was changed last minute.

I re-entered the room just as the female panel member, who had remained silent throughout, stuffed a Welsh cake into her mouth.

At that moment, I hoped she choked on it.

We reconvened and Samantha Gainard took the stand.

B: 'Miss Gainard, did you prepare your statement together with Mr Edwards?'

G: 'No'.

B: 'Your statement was made the day after Mr Edwards made his yes?'

G: 'Yes.'

B: 'In it you quote *any payment for engagement with the press would be an aggravating factor when considering the misconduct implications.* Strangely, exactly the same sentence appears in Mr Edwards's statement, word for word?'

G: 'I didn't prepare my statement alongside his.'

B: 'You hadn't seen his statement?'

G: 'No.'

B: 'You have no idea how thirty words appear in exactly the same sequence in two statements?'

G: 'I can't give you any comment I'm afraid.'

I felt myself shift in my seat. I was furious and my frustration was fighting to escape from every pore. I knew my body language was evident, my voice wasn't needed. I just wanted to scream at the blatant discrepancies. I looked at the panel, expressionless, as they clearly chose to dismiss the enormity of this.

B: 'Really? Okay, can we look at the notes you took within twenty minutes of the meeting?'

G: 'Yes.'

B: 'The words; *Jill Evans advised that she'd spoken to* The Sun *newspaper but she'd not engaged with them.* You said that was verbatim, was it?'

G: 'That's what she said.'

B: 'The word *engaged*, was that her word?'

G: 'Yes.'

Not according to me or Mr Edwards.

B: 'Miss Gainard leave your notes aside. What was

your personal recollection of the meeting? The word *engaged* was Jill Evans word was it? Not Mr Edwards?

G: 'No it was Jill Evans word.'

B: 'Have you written down in these notes of yours everything that was said?'

G: 'I wrote down the most salient.'

B: 'Can you remember exactly what was said?'

G: 'Yes!'

B: 'Okay then, can you tell us what was said immediately after she said, *I had spoken* to The Sun *newspaper but had not engaged with them.*

G: 'Well, I don't know but I have a recollection in my head I'm comfortable with.'

So, you can remember everything said, but actually you can't.

B: 'So you recall that phrase word for word, but not the next phrase, is that right?'

G: 'I can tell you the basis of the conversation, with prompting I will remember exactly.'

Ridiculous.

B: 'Well I've suggested you are wrong when you say the sentence is verbatim from Jill as it was in fact Mr Edwards who used the word 'engaged.'

G: 'No he didn't.'

B: 'Well the panel has heard from Mr Edwards already, they will make their own decision on that. So. Seeing as you have a good recollection of the meeting, there is nothing of any importance that is not contained in these notes that we should be aware of?'

G: 'There is nothing which needed to be accounted for that isn't within those notes, correct.'

Which is why Mr Edwards alleged question about 'anything else he should be made aware of 'is absent, as it was never asked.

B: 'If Jill Evans was specifically asked if there was anything else she should make Mr Edwards aware of, you would have recorded that in your notes as that would have been important?

G: 'No, he did ask that.'

B: 'Oh, he did, did he?'

G: 'Yes, but I didn't record it as she said *no*, had she said *yes* it would have been a salient point.'

Bullshit.

B: 'Your notes state the meeting concluded with Peter Dickenson confirming he would take the opportunity to discuss the issues with Jill Evans.

G: 'Yes.'

B: 'That was a matter of importance was it?'

G: 'No. That is what was said.'

So, let me be clear. You write down everything, even irrelevant details, yet you don't write down important questions. But that's because it was never asked.

B: 'Right, so why not write down what was clearly an important question, indeed if it was ever said, *Is there anything else I need to be made aware of*?

G: 'Because a negative answer was given.'

B: 'And the direct response from Mr Edwards was that any response to a newspaper or magazine, would be a matter for Sergeant Evans that was made perfectly clear?'

G: 'He can't tell her not to engage with a newspaper. That would have been a matter for herself as to whether she chose to engage with them or not.'

B: 'Mr Edwards could tell her as a police officer couldn't he?'

G: 'I don't know.'

B: 'You can't engage with the media? You are the Force lawyer.'

G: 'I don't know.'

I rubbed my face with my hands trying to make sense of her evidence. So, in summary you did not see Mr Edwards's statement, despite parts being identically worded to your own, 'engage' was Sergeant Evans' word, despite Mr Edwards stating it was his, and you only wrote down salient notes - and yet include a non-salient note about Mr Dickenson. And you, as the force lawyer, don't know whether a senior officer can give a lawful command?

Unbelievable.

B: 'No further questions, Ms Gainard.'

I left that day feeling totally drained and disillusioned. Both Edwards and the solicitor had been caught out and my team were upbeat. But I knew this didn't bode well. The force and panel knew that if their evidence got out into the public domain it wouldn't reflect well on the integrity, or rather lack of it, from its senior officers, plus they still had the problem of me on their hands, associated with an armed robber. The bad publicity the force had received over Mr Grange meant that to add more senior officers to the mix would be a catastrophe. The loss of a sergeant, however, would be an excellent result. Especially with the one-sided view, already out there, that I must have known, and was a 'bent' copper. My dismissal would make me disappear and leave their murky 'integrity' intact.

22

In my Mind I was there

The next day arrived almost as quickly as the previous seemed to end, and I found a strange solace driving in the early morning gloom. The trees, stripped bare of leaves, looked skeletal as their bony branches created a tunnel-like canopy over the long black road ahead. I drove as if on auto pilot towards the distant black clouds, their fluffy edges highlighted by the surreal early-morning blancmange pink sky.

My mind tried to summarise the events of the previous day. I struggled to understand why those people, with their status, could behave so badly. It was not in my blood to act in that way and why it was so easy for others to do so I could not fathom. Did they really despise me that much? Was my expulsion worth that? And what was that business with Acting Chief Edwards about? That me and my problems were so big that had he showed weakness the other senior ranks would fold. What the hell was the matter with them? They were supposed to be men of strength with great leadership skills. In my view they were neither. Despite everything I was dealing with, I was still standing and I had more strength in my little finger than the lot of them put together.

I had failed to reach an answer by the time I turned into the car park and parked my thoughts along with the car.

I composed myself for another long day.

First up, Chief Superintendent Dean Richards. My barrister hit the ground running.

B: 'Ok so when you took the post of Divisional Commander you had already been 'indoctrinated' into Jill's circumstances. That is the word you used in your statement.'

Yes, indoctrinated, to accept a set of beliefs; their beliefs as opposed to the truth.

DR: 'Correct, yes.'

B: 'A few days before the *Sun* news article she came to you didn't she?'

DR; 'Yes, she told me she'd been approached by reporters with regards to her relationship with Jenkins.'

B: 'And she told you they said they had information to run a story.'

DR: 'I can't remember her saying that.'

Here we go again, why do all these senior officers have a problem with their memories?

B: 'Did you make a memo?'

DR: 'No I didn't.'

B: 'You say in your statement you have a practice of making memos, why didn't you make one about this conversation?'

DR: 'I can't explain, I have a practice of making memos, but perhaps not 100% of the time.'

B: 'You told her you were glad she'd come to talk to you about it, right?'

DR: 'I can't recall that.'

B: 'That would make sense wouldn't it? You'd been briefed regarding Jill and would have been glad she'd come to you?'

DR: 'Well I would have expected her to as I was the Divisional Commander.'

B: 'But you told her the press was a decision for her?'

DR: 'I don't think I used those words.'

B: 'Do you remember she told you she had been contacted by the newspapers and she was concerned as she had a Facebook account and her photos could be accessed?'

DR: 'I don't recall that, no.'

B: 'But you recall something about Facebook?'

DR: 'I do, yeah.'

B: 'You haven't made any notes or memos in relation to that either?'

DR: 'No. I think the Facebook issue was mentioned after the article was published in the *Sun*.'

B: 'I'm going to suggest you are wrong about that and it was before the article.'

DR: 'No.'

B: 'Were you concerned and sympathetic to the predicament she found herself in?'

DR: 'To a certain extent, yes.'

B: 'And you told her this didn't you?'

DR: 'No.'

B: 'You told her in one respect it would be a good thing if it came out in the press because it would relieve the pressure if it was out there?'

DR: 'Certainly not, certainly not, I did not say that.'

You did.

His tone started to change, and I detected an air of defence, his chubby cheeks reddening as fast as a chameleon changes colour.

DR: 'I've got twenty six years in this force and there is no way I would have said for her to engage with the press...or...or whatever words you used.'

Engaged. That word again. Just four years to go before retirement, and you are not prepared to accurately recall or risk going against the other senior officers in the name of truth, otherwise your grabbing hands will not get their grip on a nice big promotion, pension and lump sum.

B: 'Well there is nothing wrong with saying that is there? Nothing wrong in *per se* speaking to the press?'

DR: 'I didn't say it so I don't know how you know this.'

B: 'You said if it came out you would support her and it would eventually calm down and be yesterday's news. That is what you told her.'

DR: 'No.'

Beads of sweat glistened on his forehead.
Body language speaks volumes when words won't.

B: 'You spoke to her before the Service confidence meeting? Correct?'

DR: 'Correct, yes.'

B: 'And she told you she'd signed a contract with a magazine and that there had been an earlier meeting with Mr Edwards?'

DR: 'Yes.'

B: 'And that Mr Edwards had said that if she cooperated with the press and received a fee as a result, there could be a disciplinary investigation.'

DR: 'That's what she told me, yes.'

B: 'You have previously worked in Professional Standards Mr Richards?'

DR: 'Correct.'

B: 'When she told you what Mr Edwards had said to her, what paragraph of the Code of Conduct do you think Mr Edwards was talking about being breached?'

DR: 'Well I wouldn't be able to answer that.'

B: 'No! Because when she told you about this you didn't understand, you were bemused by the reference to disciplinary proceedings weren't you? In fact you leaned back in your chair, arms behind your head, telling her to make a bit of money for young Frankie?'

That's exactly what you did. I remember every movement, even the movement of the chair. You always remember things that strike an emotion.

DR: 'No! I don't think I've thought about discipline proceedings and what particular Code of Conduct.'

B: 'And you told her in fact that you couldn't see what conduct she had been breaching?'

DR: 'No. No. No!

B: 'She in fact asked you to raise the issue with the magazine at the Service Confidence meeting, didn't she?'

DR: 'She said she was aware there was a meeting due.'

B: 'And she wanted you to raise it with them...we'll get there slowly Mr Richards...'

DR: 'Correct.'

B: 'And so it was clear she was looking for advice from you and the panel at that meeting?'

DR: 'No, no she hadn't told Mr Edwards on the Friday and I think she'd thought about it on the weekend and thought someone should know about it and so came to my office.'

If I was out to deceive anyone, why would I go to the trouble of telling you?

B: 'Well, I'd say it was clear she was looking for advice because when you spoke to the panel later that day you told them she was unsure whether the contract was binding in the event she withdrew her cooperation, hence her asking the question.'

DR: 'I wouldn't say she was looking for advice, she just wanted me to bring to the attention of the group that she had signed for this magazine.'

Again, why would I do that if I was looking to mislead and manipulate you all? I simply wouldn't tell you.

B: 'Let's look an office memo you did make: *PS Evans stated that she felt she had signed a contract and would have to cooperate with the article; however, she would not take payment.*

B: 'That's not what was said was it, that wasn't what she said in the meeting with you?'

DR: 'Well, that's what I've recorded.'

B: 'Because you told the panel, and you've already confirmed the minutes are fair and accurate: *She was not sure whether or not the contract was binding on her in the event of her withdrawing her cooperation.*

B: There is a difference isn't there Mr Richards?'

DR: 'I can't see the difference?'

B: 'Well there is a clear difference! One says she is not sure whether the contract is binding on her in the event of withdrawal. The other says she felt she would have to cooperate with the article. There is an obvious difference in your memo and the minutes of the meeting.'

DR: 'I don't know.'

It is obvious.

B: 'In fact you gave her some guidance and told her

in your view it was better to cooperate with the magazine and try control what was written.'

DR: 'Look I categorically deny that, I would never say that.'

You would and you did.

B: 'And you said it would be five minutes of fame and it would blow over.'
DR: 'I did not.'

Yes. You did.

B: 'And that, Mr Richards, is why she made reference to fame when she emailed you the following day trying to find a result from the meeting.'
DR: 'I was astounded at the tone of the email and its informality. I've no relation with her other than Divisional Commander and so that's why I then went to her office to discuss it?

B: 'The tone of the email reflects the tone of the meeting you had with her? Low key, relaxed.'
DR: 'Do you want me to say no again?'
B: 'The email reads: *Apologies bothering you. I appreciate you cannot discuss the contents of the meeting yesterday, I can probably guess. However I was wondering if you had any feedback re what we discussed. I am*

expecting a phone call later this evening and apparently 'fame' but not the 'fortune' bit now beckons.

B: 'Anyone reading this email will think that is a follow on, the tone is exactly the same as Jill had with you the previous day Mr Richards and how she describes the exchange in her statement?'

DR: 'No.'

B: 'And if you look at the Service Confidence minutes there was nothing that we now find out that was misleading at all. She asked for advice.'

DR: 'I don't know...I don't know what you are getting at, sir?'

B: 'Well, point out to me any bit which she had told you and you told the panel, which has turned out to be misleading or wrong?'

DR: 'No, there is nothing misleading or wrong in what she said.'

B: 'So everything she told you on that day has in fact turned out to be perfectly accurate?'

DR: 'Yes.'

Yet everything you senior officers have to say has been perfectly inaccurate.

B: 'And I asked you Mr Richards about your approach at this meeting with Jill and I said your approach was much friendlier than you will accept and you said you were guarded as you needed to clarify with Mr Edwards exactly what was said. But you haven't done that?'

DR: 'Well, I've not had a conversation with Mr Edwards.'

B: 'We know that, as we can see the panel decided to seek advice on the position and it was because of that that your tone did change with Sergeant Evans when you spoke to her the following day. That is when you simply said the situation was the same as when Edwards had spoken to her and warned her *to tread very carefully.*

Yes, as after the meeting you were panicking that your initial approach would get you into hot water, thus your tone became more formal and compliant with what you had learned at the meeting. You were covering your own ass.

DR: 'No. What I did say was I don't think you realise how serious this is judging by the email.'

Is he for real? Why would I send an email, in that tone, out of the blue?

B: 'Anyone reading that email would think it's a follow on from the tone of a previous conversation, albeit to try and comfort her, offer her sympathy and support. In fact, the day after the meeting and shortly after this email was sent, you visited her in her office did you not?

DR: 'I can't recall.'

B: 'You showed her an email from the *Trisha* show.'

DR: 'I can't recall that.'

B: 'Do you remember seeing an email from the *Trisha* show?'

DR: 'I do, yes, as it was subject to an issue at the police station.'

B: 'It was an issue because Jill complained when you showed her, it had been sent around with inappropriate comments?'

DR: 'Correct'.

B: 'And Jill was upset.'

DR: 'Correct.'

B: 'And she broke down in tears when you showed her.'

DR: 'I don't recall that meeting.'

More memory loss.

B: 'No, so why would she react in that way while shortly before sending you an email, light-heartedly referencing *fame and fortune* if it wasn't something you had mentioned?'

Silence.

Because *fame and fortune* were your original words. And your silence speaks volumes.

B: 'Thank you, Mr Richards. 'The next witness is Chief Superintendent Amphlett.'

I rubbed my face furiously with both hands and took a deep breath. I returned to the question I had mulled over on my journey that morning: How could they be so shifty? In fact, how could they be so stupid? Anyone could see they were being untruthful, and while I wanted to gasp and scream every time they did so, the panel appeared unmoved. It was my hearing. A test of my honesty and integrity and yet every senior officer to date had been caught out under cross examination. It was a farce. How could an organisation I had loved, respected and served for seventeen years harbour such gangrenous and corrupt behaviour from those who should set an example? How did I, or more worryingly, the public, ever stand a chance against people like this? And the irony? I had apparently *manipulated* them all. Me. A sergeant.

Ordinarily I would have taken that as a compliment but to be associated with such vile individuals made me feel nothing but repulsion and shame. I no longer felt proud of the force I had served.

B: 'Mr Amphlett I want to cast you back to the first meeting that Kent Police had with Jill at her home, you were not present at that meeting and not aware therefore what was said?'

PA: 'Correct.'

B: 'You did become aware after the meeting a decision was made that Jill would not be making a statement?'

PA: 'Yes.'

B: 'It wasn't the other way around? It wasn't from the off she said she wasn't going to give a statement, it was a decision made at the meeting?'

PA: 'Yes I was informed after the meeting a statement would not be given on the advice of the Federation.'

My advice. My right.

B: 'Did Kent express any concerns with Jill following this meeting?'

PA: 'They were frustrated they could not get a statement.'

B: 'What did you do about that?'

PA: 'I don't think I did anything but I later tried to broker a meeting between them both.

B: 'You had no idea Kent were coming down on the 18th of the month, in fact this was a day Jill was at the prison with Peter Dickenson?'

PA: 'No.'

B: 'Neither did Jill Evans?'

PA: 'I believe not.'

Yet this was one of the days I was deemed

uncooperative.

B: 'She wouldn't have done would she as you were the point of contact?'

PA: 'Correct.'

B: 'They said they had put together a list of questions they wanted to put to her.'

PA: 'Yes.'

B: 'And the meeting was to be conducted at a neutral venue at Jill's request. Anything unusual in that?'

PA: 'No.'

B: 'And you said in your statement it happened in this very room.'

PA: 'I had the impression it was in this room but it may not have been.'

It was not in this room; it was a different room.

B: 'Okay your statement. *I agreed to facilitate the meeting and following contact with Peter Dickenson it was apparent she initially did not want to meet the Kent officers who were becoming increasingly frustrated by her lack of cooperation. Jill turned up late for the meeting. Peter Dickenson also attended and I arrived independently. The Kent officers attempted to ask questions from the prepared list but it was not a particularly productive meeting. Jill was very defensive. I do not think the officers managed to get through all the*

*questions and no statement was obtained from Jill. I
considered the conduct of the Kent officers was
professional throughout the meeting. At no time would I
describe their conduct as bullying or overbearing.*

I was legally entitled to decline meeting the Kent
officers, to avoid being used as a witness.

I was not late for the meeting; we arrived at the
same time.

B: 'You weren't at the meeting though were you Mr
Amphlett?'

PA: 'Yes I was.'

B: 'No, you were not.'

I watched him carefully, this was the point where I
expected him to start squirming because he had been
found out.

PA: 'In my mind I was there.'

You are the lead in Operations of this force, should
a major incident occur, you are the man in charge.
But the public need not fear as even if you are not at
the incident, you have the ability to be there in 'your
mind'.

I couldn't believe what I had just heard tumbling
from his mouth.

There was an uneasy pause within the room.

B: 'What do you mean, *in your mind*?'

PA: 'Well, I brokered the meeting. In my mind I was there throughout the meeting, but I wasn't really.'

Sighs around the room.

I rested my forehead on the desk before me in despair and banged it, once.

B: 'Do you accept your statement is misleading?'

PA: 'There is no lie.'

It's a lie.

B: 'It's misleading.'

PA: 'Well it is incorrect hence there is a subsequent statement made.'

No, it is definitely a lie.

B: 'But the subsequent statement was obtained after Professional Standards came back and pointed out an issue with your statement when Jill pointed it out?'

PA: 'Yes.'

B: 'You didn't volunteer it?'

PA: 'No, I felt I was at that meeting.'

B: 'And if it hadn't been established through other sources that you weren't there you would never have made that second statement correcting it?'

PA: 'Probably not, no.'

B: 'And you understand what you have written about Sergeant Evans is misleading? In fact, it's one of her charges?'

PA: 'Yes certainly incorrect.'

So again, why am I charged with it?

B: 'You say that the conduct of the Kent officers was professional whereas Jill was defensive? That is misleading.'

PA: 'Yes.'

B: 'You were told after the meeting that Jill had not answered all the questions on the list?'

PA: 'Yes, by Kent officer Andrea Bishop.'

B: Ah, the statement of Andrea Bishop: *We went through the list of questions prepared and she did answer all the questions we put to her.* Also Peter Dickensons statement, now he **was** present at the meeting: *Jill fully cooperated with the Kent officers who acknowledged that fact. Jill answered all questions put to her. None of the questions were a surprise, in fact, some were a repeat from the initial interview. The officers asked Jill if they knew how Dean intended to plead and could she tell them as soon as she knew. I considered this request to be unprofessional and Jill made it clear that Dean's plea was a matter for him and his legal advisors.'

B: 'You suggested to her there might be a risk of her

being arrested?'

PA: 'Yeah, if she didn't attend.'

B: 'No Kent officers though ever suggested they were looking to arrest Jill?'

PA: 'They didn't say to me specifically that they intended to arrest her.'

B: 'No, they treated her as a witness and they didn't see her as complicit to criminal offences.'

PA: 'Yes.'

B: 'The senior investigating officer for Kent's statement reads: *She did answer my team's questions, at no time did I categorise her as a suspect of the investigation.* Also, Mr Grange statement is clear: *I was aware that Sgt Evans was cooperating with Kent.* However, interesting to note, the word *cooperating* has been clumsily altered in pen to *not cooperating,* I am not quite sure by whom or why?'

Silence.

I looked immediately at Superintendent Evans. His head remained down.

B: Peter Dickenson's statement: *I met with Detective Superintendent Evans who told me he had seen a list of questions Kent Police had prepared and it was in Jill's best interests to meet with them. If she didn't, they had enough to arrest her. I was stunned at this but took him at his word. I asked to see the questions but was told that was not possible. I telephoned Jill and advised her of my conversation. Jill was devastated and couldn't believe she was facing arrest as she had done nothing wrong. She reluctantly agreed to attend Police HQ but she was clearly anxious and upset. Detective Bishop made it clear, that being said, she was only being considered as a potential witness and she never had any intentions of arresting her.* So why would you say that to her?'

PA: 'I don't know.'

B: 'You don't know.'

Because you are all bullies. You thought you could frighten me with your threats simply because I exercised my legal right. Telling me my children would be motherless for Christmas, that there were new questions to answer when there were none. Same questions which got the same answers. Nothing new.

B: 'You became aware of the *Sun* article when you were about to go into the Corporate Strategy Board meeting?'

PA: 'Yes.'

B: 'Was it brought to your attention by Mr Edwards?'

PA: 'I cannot remember specifically?'

B: 'Mr Edwards made a light hearted comment about it as he opened the meeting?'

PA: 'I certainly can't remember that.'

B: 'No more questions Mr Amphlett.'

After a short break, I was the last person to give evidence.

As I waited, my hands were shaking as I tried to compose myself. I didn't want to cry, but I felt like I was holding back a dam full of tears and suspected that this last stand, as it were, was not going to be an easy one for me.

'Sit down Sergeant Evans.'

As I did so, I looked at the panel members before me. Only the chair made eye contact, the others kept their heads down. The room was hot and stuffy from all the bodies crammed within it. It seemed like every man and his dog had turned up from Professional Standards to watch this part of the 'show', jostling for a ringside seat.

The room was silent, a few low coughs could be heard before the door opened and Superintendent Evans entered, and casually dragged a chair up next to me. He sat down, in a waft of stale smoke, with a large note pad and pen at the ready in his apparent yellow, as if nicotine stained, fingers. I looked at him and swallowed before looking questioningly at my barrister who immediately jumped to his feet.

B: 'Before we begin, may I ask the necessity for Chief Superintendent Evans to be positioned so close to my client, and the reason for his sudden appearance?'

Simultaneously my federation representative added, 'With respect, sir, I would like to ask the same question. In my vast experience of disciplinary hearings, I have never seen this before.'

The panel mumbled in low voices.

Panel: 'Prosecution is there any particular reason for this?'

Prosecution: 'Uhm, well, no. He is simply taking notes, not a great problem is it?'

Panel: 'Sergeant Evans, do you have any objections?'

JE: 'Yes, with respect, I do. He makes me feel uncomfortable and I feel intimidated.'

A communal sigh echoed from the prosecution's side.

Panel: 'Okay well taking that into account, I suppose, Chief Superintendent, we will ask you to leave the room.'

I glanced my eyes to the left and looked at him. He let out a loud huff of air, awkwardly shuffled his things together and flounced out of the room.

The Prosecution barrister (PB) rose to his feet and I braced myself.

This is going to be brutal.

Within seconds of the questions beginning, the tear flood defences melted, and a box of tissues appeared on the table in front of me.

He flung his accusations at me. Cold.

Unsympathetic. Simply doing the job he was paid handsomely for.

PB: 'Sergeant Evans, you should have known shouldn't you from an early stage that Jenkins was not the sort of person a serving officer should associate themselves with?'

JE: 'Why would that be?'

PB: 'Well now his 'Guvnor Range' contained many references to crime and specifically armed robbery?'

JE: 'It was sold legitimately in many of the major supermarkets.'

PB: 'Well let me tell you what is so obvious to anyone with an ounce of sense. He was clearly advertising what he did for a living on his men's grooming range and your *training* and *experience* should have alerted you to that.'

I laughed, exasperated, and the panel members looked up, sternly.

JE: 'With respect, sir, if you are suggesting that he would advertise his armed robbery activities on a bottle of shower gel and expect anyone, unsuspecting, to think that he actually is an armed robber, that is utterly ridiculous. Would a murderer advertise himself in the newspapers, or maybe in the local jobcentre? I really don't think so.'

PB: 'And then there is the cash he brought with him

to France.'

JE: 'Yes.'

PB: 'Well, that was another sign.'

JE: 'He is a businessman. He was used to being around people who paid thousands for a dinner bill. That was normal to him. He was used to dealing with large amounts of money in the business. I had seen it with my own eyes in Italy. Carrying cash in envelopes, which in his world was not a great amount, was therefore not at all suspicious.'

PB: 'Nevertheless it was a sign.'

I shook my head

PB: 'And then we have the lack of cooperation with Kent officers. The detective constables told you to have no contact with Jenkins yet you continued to do so.'

JE: 'I followed all the instruction I was given from my chief constable. He confirmed that in his statement. I had no support or guidance from other senior management, despite desperately asking. Mr Grange was the only one giving me any guidance.'

PB: 'Hmm well, what can't be understood is why you would even want to speak with him again?'

JE: 'If your wife was leading a double life and you found out, are you telling me you would never speak to her again and you would disassociate yourself from her the minute you discovered it?'

PB: 'Well...I'm asking the questions here Sergeant Evans.'

JE: 'I needed answers. I was sixteen weeks pregnant, not that as a man you would know anything about that. I needed to know why he had lied to me. We now have a son together.'

PB: 'Yes the fact you have produced his child has made the situation post arrest very difficult indeed...now-'

I cut in sharply

JE: 'That *child*, if you don't mind, is my *son*.'

PB: 'Well, it is the case Sergeant Evans that you have used the fact you have a son together to mask the relationship with Jenkins so that you can continue to see him.'

I looked at him and shook my head, bemused.

JE: 'Dean Jenkins is incarcerated in prison, likely to be for a long time. We have no relationship as such and haven't done since the day of his arrest. Our every move is monitored. But we do have our son and Dean is his father. Both have rights.'

PB: 'And you continued to visit against the orders of Kent.'

JE: 'Kent officers are Detective Constables. A rank below me. The Chief Constable is the ultimate authority. I believed that following his advice I could not go far wrong, but how wrong I was. His senior management team was unable to offer me any guidance or support despite being asked, on times even begged, but they set me up to fail. One minute speaking to the press is *a matter for me*, the next I am charged with a misconduct offence for doing exactly that.'

I could feel the anger beginning to bubble. The glowing ember inside me was igniting.

Calm it down, Jill.

PB: 'The fact remains you failed to cooperate with them and obstructed them in their duties?'

JE: 'I listened to my federation advisor and exercised my legal rights to avoid being dragged into court. I did the same when asked by Dean's defence team to supply a photo of him. I declined. Kent visited without my knowledge or prior arrangement and that was deemed uncooperative? I unfortunately can't read minds, unlike Mr Amphlett. He says I was obstructive and didn't answer all the questions. Kent confirmed I answered all the questions, nothing new from the first set, yet he said if I didn't meet them I would be arrested. More lies.'

I was angry now and the tears stung my face.

PB: 'Your own brother says you tried to stop him making a statement.'

JE: 'According to Kent, who were annoyed that I wasn't dancing their tune My brother and I are not close and his inaccuracy would not surprise me in the slightest. It's what he does.'

PB: 'The press. You cooperated with them.'

JE: 'As far as I could yes, but there was only so much I could do, sensational headlines sell papers. I was desperately trying to correct the incorrect stories circulating.'

PB: 'Yes, you were rather enjoying this weren't you?'

JE: 'Oh yes, delighted that my personal and professional worlds had been blown up while I was sixteen weeks pregnant. No support. No guidance. Hung out to dry.'

PB: 'No need to be flippant Sergeant Evans.'

JE: 'My apologies, it is very hard to sit here and listen to you speaking with the benefit of hindsight. So easy. You have never walked a day in my shoes for the last two years and I don't think any of you here today would still walk this earth if you had. So forgive my exasperated tone but I think I am more than justified.'

PB: 'Hmm...well, the magazine article has you talking about Dean as your *partner*.'

JE: 'Was'.

PB: 'And you are planning a future together'.

JE: 'Was. The article was changed from what was agreed. When the payment thing was sprung on me I couldn't get out of the contract and they went to press with it as they couldn't get hold of me to final check it. But we kept a copy of the originally agreed piece and you have that and it shows it to be different. And again, Professional standards had the opportunity to see the article on my behalf prior to publishing and they declined. I would suggest they wanted it to run, to *fit* their jumped up charges.'

PB: 'Where is the Mini car?'

JE: 'What Mini car?'

PB: 'Well, if we look at the photos on your phone...'

Oh, God. No!

PB: 'There is a picture of a Mini with number plate J777 GUV. Where have you hidden that vehicle? In a lock up?'

I thought for a minute, then realised the ludicrousness of what he was suggesting.

JE: 'That is a picture from the DVLA website. There is a facility to see what a number plate looks like on a vehicle. That is my plate, but I didn't buy a Mini, it's assigned to my current vehicle.'

PB: 'Are you sure, I would suggest it's hidden in a lock up somewhere?'

JE: 'Ridiculous, good luck with that one.'

I dropped my head and my voice was now low. Resigned. I shook my head

PB: 'And finally, it's true isn't it you have misled and manipulated these poor senior officers with regard to Jenkins and the media?'

JE: 'They didn't like that I had direct access to Chief Constable Grange whose statement confirms his approach was not shared by a number of senior officers. Once Mr Grange was ousted, his statement was given no value. He never lied about me. Have I been caught lying in my hearing today? No, unlike your witnesses who should hang their heads in shame. I wonder how many of them will face discipline now? Had they been PC's or Sergeants, Chief Superintendent Evans there from Professional Standards would be rubbing his paws in glee at his sudden gift of guaranteed investigations.'

I gulped in the warm, stuffy air and wiped a mixture of nasal mucus and tears roughly away from my face with my hand, before continuing.

'I will lay another bet on the verdict today which was decided long before I took the stand. Well, go ahead, do your worst. I am sick of telling the truth while those who think their rank affords them the privilege to lie.' I took a mouthful of oxygen and gulped deeply. 'Everything I have ever done, Peter Dickenson knew about and he has confirmed that, as did the Chief. This was not liked by the other senior officers who *I* believe felt that I went over their heads. But I had no choice as they were incapable of dealing with my situation and giving me any sound advice. I trusted Peter and I trusted the Chief. Peter was advising me and has put in his statement, where's my notes, oh here, look if I may read-'

PB: 'Well, don't think we need---.'

I raised my voice over his: '*I too hold the view that if anyone has brought the Force into disrepute it is Chief Officers in their backtracking and subsequent failure to honour commitments when Jill asked for support and guidance. I honestly believe that if Mr Grange had not left this organisation then Jill would not be in the position she is currently facing. In conclusion I believe Sergeant Jill Evans has been treated unfairly since the departure of Mr Grange. I do not believe her suspension is justified and I have a view there may be an abuse of process in respect of her charges and subsequent investigation.* Peter wouldn't put a bold statement in writing if he didn't believe it to be true, as with this Force everything has consequences, well, that is if you are not part of the *club*. And I'm definitely not a member of that club and would never wish to be!'

PB: 'No more questions, Sergeant Evans, you seem very agitated.'

I stood, my body shaking, as the panel filed out.

My barrister loosened his tie and collapsed into the chair; 'Well, that was a surprise. All guns blazing girl. Excuse the pun! I'm not sure how that will go down?'

'Are you not?' I said, 'I will be guilty. They have to protect the liars up the food chain and, let's face it, I am the easy solution. They have dodged a bullet with Mr Grange by throwing me to the wolves, so it's simple now isn't it? Guilty. Senior officers' integrity remain intact, the inconsistencies of this kangaroo court will be hidden, and the whole problem of Jill Evans will disappear. Just you watch.'

Within an hour, I was summoned back inside.

Chair of the Panel: 'Please stand Sergeant Evans while the verdict is given.'

As he started to read I knew what was coming. 'The panel is of the view that Sergeant Dickenson has not done you any favours. He has described the Service Confidence procedure as a *crock of shit* and has said that as he has thirty years' service he can say what he likes. He repeatedly accused senior officers of lying without providing proof.'

You witnessed the proof. What more do you need?

Chair: 'You Sergeant Evans have been poorly advised and you should have cooperated unreservedly without conditions.'

I did. So, according to you I have no rights, yet in law I actually do.

Chair: 'Your relationship with Jenkins is incompatible with your job and you have engaged with the media and thus brought your Force into disrepute, while manipulating senior officers. Therefore we find all charges substantiated and you are required to resign with immediate effect.'

I have brought the force in to disrepute!?

Panel: 'We feel it only fair to point out that there are lessons to be learned for Dyfed Powys Police in their handling of the case. Management of Sergeant Evans was not helped by the inconsistent views of the senior officers.'

And their lies. Yet I am guilty.

Panel: 'If you wait Ms Evans you can sign this form.'
So quickly I became a Ms.
JE: 'With respect, I am not wasting any more time here.'

I nodded to my team for their futile efforts and

opened the door, listening as the seal sucked it shut behind me, vacuum packing the rotten contents within.

23

Treading Water

I walked along the driveway of Police headquarters for the very last time and I held my head up high. There were no tears, no drama. I stepped with purpose and reflection.

It did not matter that I had told the truth. There was only ever going to be one verdict because that is what suited them. No matter what they labelled me with their jumped-up charges, it was not me squirming in the chair. I would carry the names of those officers that betrayed me forever, but would I spend the rest of my life simmering with anger and revenge?

No.

I had witnessed many who had taken that track and it was one that only ended in depression, self-destruct, and sometimes the extermination of a valuable life. My flame still burned; they had failed to extinguish it completely. I just needed to gently fan it now, to slowly defrost my frozen heart and crack its calcified encasement.

My thoughts turned to my children who needed me back minus the stress, frustration and tears.

I wasn't the first policeman or -woman who had been stabbed in the back and certainly wouldn't be the last.

I was simply a number. Or had been.

I pulled the collar of my black woollen coat up around my neck, plunged my hands into my deep pockets and smiled.

My son. The bastards wanted me to get rid of him. That is one decision that I got perfectly right.

I had predicted that should this day come I would be inconsolable, desolate and lost. I was wrong. The relief poured over me like a soothing elixir. I had come to the end of two years of misery. Two long years of continued relentless suffering. Pressure. Torment. My whole world obliterated by the two very things I loved and had trusted.

Dean and the Dyfed Powys Police.

Enough.

I was ready to rise from the black pit. No longer

would those who betrayed me, consume me. This verdict would not define me.

That night for the first time in months, I slept deeply.

The new day dawned with reality. I scrutinised my finances and cancelled any direct debits that were luxuries. Dean's car bill had made a large dent in my rainy-day fund but I had enough set aside to cover me for a few months out of work. My priority was the house and making sure that there were no noticeable changes to everyday life for the children. We would have to cut down on things like hair and nails, well they'd never been a priority, and as long as there was food on the table and a roof over our heads, we would be fine.

I would make sure of it. My salary stopped forthwith but I had always been a good saver and I had a bit put by. I also cashed in some Police Federation Savings Plans.

I also tried to find the elusive gossips who were suggesting that Dean had apparently buried his ill-gotten gains in the back garden so they could provide me with the map where X marks the spot. I didn't need it.

One afternoon my parents had bought me a new garden shed for my birthday. Dad had dismantled the old rotten one and was digging a new footing while Mum was helping me clear the soil away. As he thrust the shovel into the rich smelling soil, alive with juicy fat worms, there was a loud tinny thud as the shovel struck something still buried. My parents stopped and looked at each other questioningly before looking at me with furrowed brows.

'Shit', I said with the most serious face.

'What?' my mother responded, tentatively.

'Dean was digging there before he was arrested, it must be the stolen money the police think I have hidden away.'

My mother wobbled as all the colour drained from her face and she felt for the decking to sit down.

'Oh, God', she squeaked, as my father dragged the metal tin from the soggy hole. He prized the rusty lid open as my mum covered her face with her hand and peered through her open fingers.

The remains of the dead cat did not amount to the alleged 'stashed fortune' though I am sure had Dyfed Powys Police been investigating the cat would have been sent for a post mortem to establish whether they could arrest me for the murder of 'Tiddles'.

Life slowly returned to a new kind of normal. I claimed benefits for the first time in my life and hated it with a passion so quickly began looking for jobs. I had to keep moving forward and simultaneously trained up as a mobile beauty spray tanning technician. I worked evenings from home and put in long hours. Within a short space of time I built up a clientele list and it did the job it was designed to do. It kept the wolves from the door.

One evening the phone rang and I answered it. 'Hello?'

There was a pause on the other end

'Hello Darlin', how are you doing?'

Dean.

I took a deep breath as my heart lurched.

'Hey, I'm okay, surprisingly. I'm no longer a police officer, your gang and my gang put paid to that. But I'm getting there.'

'I am so sorry Jill. They are bastards.'

'Don't exclude yourself from that description Dean. I have wasted enough air on the subject, and I am moving forward.'

'If I send you a visiting order will you come with Frankie?'

'Yes, I will Dean, I will come with Frankie.'

Two weeks later I found myself once again at the gates of the prison. As I waited to go in, I recalled my first visit and my thoughts on how alien I felt, and still did.

People like me had no choice but to get used to prison environment if loved ones made those decisions that imposed consequences on the lives of unsuspecting others.

As I walked into the visiting room Dean stood up, still in the netball bib. Time, it seemed, stood still in there.

He held his arms out and this time I allowed them

to encase me. I hadn't wanted to be hugged by anyone other than by my children in a very long time and, whatever I thought of him, support at that time meant everything. He was all I knew.

'I'm so sorry things worked out this way.'

'Let's not go back down that road anymore… how's life with you?'

I stepped back and studied him in silence. As he spoke, words were little compensation. I wondered whether anywhere in the orbit of his mind, he had realised how many lives he would ruin through the choices he made. The reply to this now pointless question, either way would not change things and would be of no benefit to anyone. Nothing could reverse the seed of mistrust, planted by his own hand that had germinated and rooted itself deep within my soul, spreading faster than a Japanese Knotweed.

Could things ever be the same? Trust is a very powerful thing, once broken it's rarely fixable. The only cure is complete removal.

A decision that is difficult for the head and heart to harmonise.

I agreed to bring Frankie when I could but made no promises to myself for the future beyond those walls. On good days, I liked to immerse myself back into the love of the relationship, we would laugh, dream about our plans for the future but then on the lonely drive home, days when I could literally sleep at the wheel, that nagging voice would return. Is this what you really want? Is this the way you will spend your life? Balanced on this knife's edge for more than seven long years?

I trusted nobody. Not even myself.

My parents took my requirement to resign badly. Relations had remained far more distant with them since the incident with my brother, and I had not conversed with him since. There was often an atmosphere when I visited, and it wasn't long before the blame game started from my father, how my refusal to trust the police and do as I was told, regardless of my rights or their integrity, had cost me my job. My mother was different and deep down I knew she disagreed but kept the peace because of my father. Mum offered to support me financially, but I refused as I had never asked for money in my life and wasn't about to start then. If I couldn't afford it, I simply would not have it. I was struggling financially but I would find a way through it.

Within months a job came up with the local council. I applied and was shortlisted for the interview, which appeared to go very well. Until the question I most dreaded, arose.

'Why did you leave your job with the police?'

I had given this some thought. 'I was required to resign due to personal circumstances beyond my control.'

'Oh, okay…we didn't expect that answer but thank you for being so honest, not many are.'

Tell me about it.

Within days I was offered the job and I was over the moon. I was back in the elevator, heading skywards.

But it stalled at the first floor.

Instead of a start date, I received a letter. *We carefully reviewed your application and suitability for the post of Area Estate Warden. In light of information given in the employer's reference by Dyfed Powys Police and the necessary degree of trust this position entails and its links to external agencies, including Dyfed Powys Police, it has been decided that the offer of employment must be withdrawn.*

I held the letter in my hand and sat down slowly on the edge of my bed to absorb the new source of rejection.

You have seen this before...it's nothing new. Did you really think they would stop putting the boot in?

My logic sat on one side of the old-fashioned weighing scales, opposite pounds of simmering emotion. The scales descended in logic's favour.

Some detective skills later, it transpired that the head of the council department sat on the board of the Police Authority and word was he was a personal friend of Dean Richards. It didn't take much to put two and two together.

I was devastated. Angry. So, this was the way it was going to be, was it?

I learned quickly that to apply for any jobs

remotely linked to the police was futile. I wasn't one of the privileged rank, who miraculously had their retirement, pension and future bonus job nicely tied up.

Inspector Hayes, my 'welfare' officer with the apparent preference for 'lower standards', retired in 2009, having spent the last year of his service temporarily promoted to the dog section in HQ as a chief inspector, despite having no previous experience with the dog unit. This was a strange, but convenient move as this made way for the brother of Dean Richards to take the Chief Inspector role in Pembrokeshire and work under his older sibling as part of the senior management team. Hayes then retired, a year later, on a chief inspector's pension as opposed to that of an inspector and walked straight into a regular wage, that of a licencing officer post in the Pembrokeshire Division, where Dean Richards still held court.

Such a fortunate stroke of luck, especially as Hayes was a cousin of Richards, thus keeping nepotism firmly alive within the Force.

I was less fortunate; my family was fractured, and I was unemployed and applying via more ethical channels for jobs. One came up in sales, twenty hours per week at the Carphone Warehouse and I jumped at the chance. I had to pass a Financial Services Authority check covering honesty, integrity, reputation, competence and capability. I passed with flying colours.

I surmised that the bigger the fish I applied for; the less sabotage Dyfed Powys Police could bring.

The elevator juddered upwards.

It was while attending a training course in London that a change began, and my body began to fail. There had been early warning signs. Heart palpitations, struggling on times to catch my breath. These 'aperitif' like symptoms eventually made way for the serving of the main course. The stress of the past years began to surface, like craters rupturing, allowing pressure to eventually escape from the grumbling volcano. A full six months had passed since the hearing and this was totally unexpected. I was strong, I had always been strong so why was my body failing now?

I was travelling on a coach to the training venue when suddenly my ears started to buzz as if someone was twisting a high frequency dial. The noise was unbearable. I actually found myself looking around for the source. My breathing was laboured and as I gasped for air in panic, my mind convinced me I was going to die. The more I thought and panicked, the faster death approached. My heart thumped in my chest and my limbs felt flaccid as a cold sweat trickled down my back and my stomach churned. I couldn't hear anything but could see passenger's lips moving, before I rested my head down on my knees and willed my heart to stay with me.

I'm going to die. I'm going to die on this bus in London. Please don't let me die.

I had experienced my first panic attack.

Previously I had never been convinced by these or whether they existed and had often raised my eyes when prisoners started gasping for breath and claiming they were in the throes of one.

I have since learned that those things I've ever doubted or dismissed as nonsense, the universe has eventually thrown back at me to personally experience, learn valuable lessons from and thus grow.

This attack was the first of many and, as I began to learn the warning signs, I quickly mastered how to deal with them. As terrifying as they were, they made me understand myself that little bit more and that there were matters under my external shell that needed urgent attention.

Life was too short to waste a minute longer.

I began the rebuild and, in the process, became my own best friend.

One Saturday morning Karma paid her first visit.

As I served a customer, I could see an ex-CID colleague hovering near the budget phones. My colleague asked to assist him, but he declined, preferring to wait for me. As soon as I was free, he approached.

'Hi Jill, how are you? I'm sorry to ask but we have a

guy in custody. You dealt with him at an incident some time ago and your evidence, we know, would be good accurate evidence, crucial to convict him. Would you be willing to check your pocket notebooks and help us?'

I was stunned, my mouth dropped open like a rusty old draw bridge and out of it echoed the loudest involuntary laugh.

He stood expressionless.

'Is this a joke?'

Silence.

'It's not a joke, is it?'

He looked at me with a confused expression.

'Well…unfortunately I can't help as I apparently lack 'honesty and integrity', which prevents me from being any sort of credible witness. So, I guess that means your suspect is having an extremely lucky day.'

'Ah come on, we know all that shit they put you through was exactly that, bullshit. Can you just check your books, you know, as a favour?'

'I am all out of favours. The answer is no.'

'Well, just think about it?'

'Okay, I will.'

'Great,' he said, 'thanks Jill.'

I put my finger to my lips and looked skywards. Then I smiled. 'The answer is still no.'

He left and did not look back.

My team had lodged an appeal against my hearing

verdict, and I made misconduct complaints against Edwards and Amphlett regarding the integrity of their statements. All three complaints were dismissed and signed off with a written consolation prize: *As a learning point, the committee will emphasise to the senior officers and force the need for attention to detail when writing statements.*

That was a huge comfort.

Write a statement while holding a senior rank and be assured that if it is incorrect, you will simply be given some friendly advice. However, be of lesser rank and bring such things to light, your fate will likely result in dismissal.

Where was the integrity in that?

But there was some news.

Karma made her second visit.

The results of my complaint were in. Both forces were found to have breached Data Protection and my privacy rights in relation to the distribution of my photographs and were required to come to a compensatory agreement with a formal apology. This small, moral victory was worth its weight in gold.

Professional Standards were proved wrong and Dyfed Powys Police was not the perceived oracle of legal compliance.

24

Rock Bottom

I continued to visit Dean as and when I could, and through letter and phone conversation the subject turned to us realistically having a future together. I knew of nothing else now, I had stood by him as the weeks and months rolled into years as I believed I would never trust anyone again and felt it was probably better the devil I knew than any I didn't.

Dean was a model prisoner and was soon transferred to a category D prison in Gloucester, which made visits far easier. He became a 'listener', working with the prison officers and helping with the settlement of new inmates. He earned privileges.

This prison environment was more relaxed, more like an army camp regime, and I could pass off to a growing and inquisitive Frankie that we simply visited Daddy at work. There was a garden, a play area and not a roll of barbed wire or fortress styled walls for miles.

One Christmas I made the five hour round trip alone. Visiting ended at 4pm and my plan was to go straight to some tanning appointments on my way home. I was tired, working all hours between both jobs, and wore my pink work beauty tunic to the visit, to enable me to do so. It was a wedding booking and too much cash to turn down.

This visit marked the beginning of another change. A shift.

As Dean entered the visit room I stood up and smiled, but his reciprocal grin suddenly changed to a frown. His dark eyes looked full of fury. He sat down and leaned in to give me a kiss but instead, in a low monotone voice, whispered in my ear 'How dare you wear work uniform to visit me.'

I jolted back as if I'd been electrocuted but then realised that surely this was a joke and just his sense of humour. I laughed his comment off. 'Ah well, when you have to work all hours there is little time to be glamorous.'

'Are you listening to me? When you come to visit me, I expect you to make an effort, how dare you turn up here looking like that?' His voice was low.

I suddenly realised this was not his sense of humour and this was certainly not funny. He was serious. My mind raced.

I've travelled hundreds of miles in the dark and cold to see you. I have to work afterwards as I have to support my family at Christmas, our son. And you are concerned about me wearing a work tunic?'

I suddenly felt the old feelings of disappointment crawl all over me, as if I had let him down and upset him, while all I was trying to do was juggle many balls. A glamorous appearance was not top of my list, my clothes and make-up simple. I could feel a lump in my throat and the tears began to well, like water bombs. I looked to the guard and yet again swallowed hard, forcing the waters back.

Dean continued, 'Next time, don't bother coming here if you are dressed like that. What is wrong with you? Everyone else's Mrs has made a bleedin' effort and then there is you, for fuck's sake.'

I kept my head down and sat on my hands like a naughty child. What a mess you are, providing more disappointment wherever you go. He is upset now, how could you be so thoughtless.

I blamed myself, there was no question he was, of course, right.

The rest of the visit was strained, and it couldn't end fast enough. Conversation comprised of one-word responses from Dean and I was grateful that half an hour was spent alone, stood queuing for coffee. I tried to make up for the upset I had caused him by stretching my budget to purchasing an extra Twix bar to have with his coffee but still the atmosphere did not melt, unlike the chocolate stick he roughly stabbed into the scalding drink. It was frostier than the cold grey foggy darkness outside, which contrasted with the bright strip lighting in the stuffy visiting room.

As I returned to my car, the thud of the door closing was comforting. As the interior light dimmed, I sobbed aloud.

Something broke inside me that day.

This is not my sentence, but it may as well be. I think I've served enough.

The words of Chief Constable Grange resonated around my head: *It will take a while but eventually she will see sense and this relationship will come to an end.*

This particular train was suddenly approaching the station and I had a feeling my stop and time to alight was getting closer. I noticed Dean's letters then becoming more dictatorial. He often 'joked' that I needed to remember who was the boss, and any future plans made were his plans. Mine were secondary. The thread of doubt had metamorphosed into a rope and I started to feel resentment. Confined. And I didn't like it.

The final straw came when Dean needed a release address and naturally wanted to use mine. He explained that Social Services would need to become involved with me and the children, to establish whether it was a suitable place for him and *vice versa* for us to live together.

The train reached the end of the line and the doors slid open. It was time to step off and be honest with myself.

The phone rang.

'I can't do this anymore,' I blurted.

'What do you mean? It's been five years, and we are nearly there now.'

'I know, I'm so sorry to let you down. I'm not having my children scrutinised by Social Services and I feel we've run our course. So much hurt. So much deceit. My love for you feels like a butter dish that's empty and I'm struggling to make it cover the bread. I can't serve this sentence with you anymore Dean. I can't.'

'There's someone else isn't there.'

His voice was calm, and it was a statement as opposed to a question.

'There is nobody, but life is passing me by. I've lost so much, and I want a fresh start. A new outlook, this is just stifling me, it's a burden, I don't feel loved and I feel worthless.'

'Oh, so I'm a fucking burden now?'

I feel worthless. Unloved. Did you not hear me?

'How am I supposed to feel, banged up in here?'

I sighed. But you chose that path. I didn't. And I can no longer carry the burden with you, I've paid my dues for long enough now. My thoughts reinforced my actions.

'No, no look, it's just how I feel. For my own sanity I need to break this.'

'You can't.'

I can do this; I can free myself from this world of pain which I will never feel a part of.

'You can't do this to me.'

'I'm sorry.' At that moment I felt like I was confined within a room where the oxygen was vanishing, and I needed to get out to survive. It was a life-changing decision but the urge to make it was as involuntary as the feeling to push in childbirth.

And make it I did. Right there. Right then.

I felt like an enormous weight had suddenly lifted from my shoulders.

I was so sorry, but I had lived enough for others. I needed to look after myself, focus on my family, my job, and just worry about simple things like whether I had enough milk to make us all cocoa at night or whether to have egg and chips for tea on a Friday.

Simple was simply bliss.

My panic attacks began to retreat and the doors to the rooms within my mind began to slowly creak open, allowing the warmth of hope and normality to soothe the raw, painful scars within.

I ventured out a few months later, for the first time socially in years. I felt like I was eighteen again, slightly nervous at being seen in public but still guilty that I was living my life and Dean could not. I had no intention of meeting anyone. None at all.

Wales had just won the Grand Slam in rugby, the atmosphere in the pub was electric. I stood chatting when a friend came back from the bar and touched my shoulder. As I turned, she spoke, introducing me. 'Rod, you've met my friend Jill, haven't you?'

I looked up and my eyes locked with the biggest smile and eyes that reminded me of the cartoon character Gromit. I grinned.

Silence.

A warm protective hand entangled its fingers with mine, then the words, 'No, but I feel like I know her already.'

Having landed like a meteorite into my world, Rod's onward journey was far from easy. I found myself feeling a deeper kind of happiness flow through my veins.

But the guilt. It was unbearable.

And with that guilt came the old feelings of mistrust. I checked everything. His phone. His whereabouts. I asked more questions than a round of Mastermind, then frantically weighed up the answers to make sure everything made sense. This was nothing to do with fidelity. This was simple, raw self-preservation. If things got too close to my feelings the easiest and most natural solution was to extinguish it.

Never in my lifetime would I be fooled again.

The girls responded to Rod with mixed views. Caitlin was cold from the start and I saw a message on her mobile to Ella ridiculing Rod over a jacket he wore. It was so reminiscent of her father, a chip off the old block. She was a teenager, doing the usual teenage things; mainly holed up in a bedroom with as much dirty washing and crockery as she could hoard. Her father still continued to pour money into her and her apparent dislike for my newly found happiness was fuelled by my own father who also took an instant and unknown aversion to Rod. I initially gave them the benefit of the doubt and surmised that they were simply looking out for me, protecting me from any potential future heartache.

I later discovered that Caitlin and Ella, while visiting my parents, had made a habit of concocting tales that put Rod in a poor light and, most worryingly, were untrue.

When Rod was building me a new garage, it was transmitted that Rod was sat on the sofa doing nothing. The lies then extended to me. When asked by my parents what I had got them for birthdays or Christmas they responded that I had not bothered. They fed my parents stories that were completely untrue but which my parents believed. This caused a deepening of the chasm which consequently lost years of contact between me and my mum. My parents, dominated by my dad, sucked up everything. I suppose it seemed too far-fetched to believe my proclamations that the girls had done this deliberately but the end result was that Rod would never be accepted as part of my life, and if I chose to move forward with him, then my fate would match.

But it was my life now. Mine.

As we tried to build a new future together the cauldron continued to simmer.

I no longer felt comfortable in my home and was guarded around the girls.

It's a terrible thing to admit to yourself that you cannot trust your very own. That they would influence my own parents and turn them against me to inflict unnecessary emotional pain. It had gone far beyond protection. It was, in my eyes, deliberate. My own flesh and blood were like cuckoo fledglings, pushing me from the family nest and seemingly relishing the pain it caused me. It seemed so ridiculous that to acknowledge what was going on made me feel like I was losing my sanity. But there was no explanation. There were smiles and kindness when home but then the next trip to my parents released a devious and unkind version about events in our family home.

The tension built. With pressure from my inability to trust, old wounds were torn open and re-inflamed. My children's actions, whether unreasonable or not, I initially defended vehemently, and I began, yet again, to sacrifice my own happiness simply to keep the girls and my parents happy. I felt guilty about bringing Dean into our lives and even though I knew they had never really been affected by the aftermath, I still questioned whether their behaviour now was a result of my choices, as clearly I was incapable of making the right ones.

Plans to move in with Rod were shelved. I excluded him from family events, he wasn't welcome at my parents' home anyway. I chose when to have him in my life. My behaviour was erratic, cruel and misplaced. I cried. I stressed over the slightest thing and I blamed Rod, reinforced by everyone else, for everything that went wrong. Everything.

Except work.

Rod brought me to the attention of a property mogul he did some work for and, as a result, he asked me to manage his large property portfolio. He knew about my past and gave this response: *You are on a runway about to take off. I am not interested in what you left behind.*

Rod unlocked the door of opportunity for me and I chose to walk through. My parents view was I should remain in the safety of part-time retail, but I took the leap regardless, so too did my income along with my self-esteem and worth.

Someone actually had faith in me, accepted me at face value and, perhaps most importantly, I discovered I was still capable of courage and making good choices.

It was a spark that catalysed a slow transformation. I began to wonder whether any of the good bits of me, despite buried, remained preserved like fossils, or whether they were gone forever.

Dean was released in 2014 and relations between us were in a good place. Having served 7.5 years behind bars he admitted that being alone was actually the best and only way he could come to terms with that amount of time under lock and key. He eventually returned to the family home he had wanted to escape. Had I played the game to full time I would have found myself at the end with nothing.

I was thankful that fate had stopped the train when it did.

He began to work and contribute to Frankie, who began to know his dad in everyday life, minus the constraints of prison. That made me happy.

For me personally, I hated my reflection in the mirror. I fought a daily battle of self-doubt with a conscience that told me repeatedly how guilty I should feel for even considering a life of happiness. I was wandering a lonely wilderness, I felt betrayed by everyone, including my own children, and the very thought of how much they must hate me to inflict such hurt every time felt like a rusty saw was slicing my heart to pieces.

You are not good enough. You will never be happy. You don't deserve to be. Who else can be hated so much by her own kids and parents?

I kept this locked away, the only tell-tale leakage being when it occasionally filtered into my relationship with Rod. The mistrust. The insecurity. The waiting for the next horrific revelation. But through it all I kept the faith with Rod, and I tested it to the max.

I knew I was in trouble; my self-esteem needed some work. I sat with Rod one summer's afternoon, overlooking my favourite beach in Saundersfoot where I had spent most of my childhood at my beloved Nan's hotel.

I posed the question. 'What is the hardest physical challenge I could ever set myself?'

'Well, if you want a real mental and physical challenge, do a bodybuilding competition. But it's extremely hard, I don't think you would be able to do it.'

Hmm. I looked out at the calming power of the sea. 'Okay, I set myself a goal. One year from now I will stand on stage and compete.'

'Jill, you have a lot of muscle to build, you've never lifted weights in your life'

'Well, I had better make a start then, hadn't I?'

Twelve months later, at the age of forty-nine, I waited in the wings to walk on stage in my first competition. I felt like a phoenix rising from the flames. The transformation externally and, more importantly, internally, was huge. If I could survive years of sorrow and pain, then this moment, walking out in a bikini in a packed auditorium, would be a walk in the park. The past year had tested my physical strength and mental commitment in terms of a strict diet and brutal training regime. I lived and breathed my sport, training after long days of work and early on dark cold winter mornings, pounding the deserted winter pavements. While my body worked, my mind thoroughly processed and catalogued my life to date. Every atom of pain I recalled simply fuelled my resolve and confidence. I compared my mind to an old-fashioned cash register with the big knobbed buttons, pulling the long entry handle and banking each detail after it was correctly analysed. Each emotion, each event in its rightful storage box.

I had achieved what I set out to do. I proved to myself that nobody and nothing had broken me beyond repair. As my body got stronger, the emotional process provided the necessary fuel. I rebuilt.

I returned home that day elated. But was immediately dealt another hand.

Caitlin offered no congratulations and labelled me an 'embarrassment'. I would have loved her support and kindness, but she was so much like her father. She announced that I was no mother to her and that she would prefer the company of her dad.

She packed her things, assisted by her father, and moved in with my parents. Sometime after Ella followed suit following the emergence that she had got out of her depth with credit card bills. I had an ISA fund I had saved hard to build up and switched temporarily into her name whilst I organised my finances. This was to be split in the future between my three children. I asked Ella to close the account and transfer the money back into my name but it emerged the account was already closed and the cash spent by Ella.

She ran to my parents and denied what I had discovered as the truth. They, in turn, immediately defended her, disbelieving me despite me being armed to the hilt with the evidence.

As a result, she continued down the same spending track and I was prevented from trying to redirect her, as any parent should do, away from further trouble.

Both girls then told my parents they were forced from the family home as I had thrown them on the street for no apparent reason and taken their belongings to the local tip. My parents didn't ask for the full story, they immediately took their side and I became the villain, of course 'influenced' by Rod. Yet, their bedrooms remained as they left them, stripped of all the nice things which they had taken with them and the rubbish left for me to sort out.

My life seemed to continue with the same theme.

The girls continued with their fabrications and my parents were happy to believe. They didn't bring them home to sort matters out and, of course, the girls were reluctant as they did not want their tales exposed. They knew where they could escape challenge and get an easy life.

Parenting, whether jointly or singly, is always a difficult job. There are times where you have to be tough to put your children on the right track. Yes, they will make mistakes, but that is how they learn. My girls did not learn those vital lessons as my final expulsion from my blood family unit prevented this. Instead they were given free rein to grow into people I barely recognised or understood.

It was, of course, my fault. My dad branded the bodybuilding sport that had saved me 'seedy' which had brought them huge embarrassment, especially when my achievements were documented in the local newspaper sports column. The last time I set foot in my family home was when myself, Rod and Frankie went there, armed with evidence of the lies that had been told.

We were all three told to leave by my father.

And never to return.

As I left, I turned, and Ella smiled smugly. I sighed in disbelief, desperately wanting to help her. She was happy to escape the truth but so blissfully ignorant of what she was setting herself up for with increasing debt. It frightened me.

It seemed like every tiny piece of positivity had a sting in the tail. The foundations of my life were poured, I just needed them to set, but the price was non-negotiable.

The dark betrayal by, and the resultant estrangement of, my two children.

They truly ripped my heart in two and stamped on it. I cried rivers of tears and felt bereaved.

Birthdays, Christmas. Years passed without acknowledgement or response to messages. My mobile number was blocked on my mum's phone, so any texts, whether birthday wishes or attempts to heal the rift that I sent were, unbeknownst to me or my mother, not getting through.

Caitlin passed her A Levels, but nobody told me, or which university she chose. I missed her first day. I was cut from their lives like I never existed, with both their fathers doing nothing to heal the separation. David had re married with a family of his own so his priorities were elsewhere. Huw, still single, positively encouraged it. I received tales of him telling my mother that his advice was to have nothing to do with me. That was hard as I had never stood in the way of his relationship with Caitlin and I never believed that deep down both girls didn't miss me, or need me around. I believe they had been so poisoned that to show any love towards me would have been seen as a betrayal of loyalty toward Huw, David or to my parents, to whom they had spun their tales, and who believed them implicitly.

My fiftieth birthday passed without their acknowledgement.

I may as well have been dead to them.

The final ultimatum came via my parents. If I chose to continue the relationship with Rod and eventually marry, my father would cut me from their will.

So, another big dice was rolled in my direction from the least expected source.

Choose Rod and lose my parents and consequently my girls. Choose my parents and drive Rod away. Or, indeed, drive anyone who had the potential to bring me happiness and a new life, away. Treat Rod as I had once been treated, when I had invested trust and loyalty only to be tossed aside. Unimportant. Irrelevant. I could never do that. If the relationship with Rod was not right then I would, as would he, be honest. But that was our decision to make, never anyone else's and certainly not an axe to hang over my head.

I should never have been given that ultimatum. Who has the right to dictate another's choice and happiness? I was fifty years old, not ten. Who would do that?

My father. That's who.

Things came to a head one Sunday when I burnt my hand on the hair straighteners and reacted by smashing them and my bedroom wall, to pieces. I wanted to physically hurt myself, not in a life-threatening way, but as if the physical pain would be better than the slow torture in my head. It was release.

Rod watched and held back, as if he knew this needed to play out, before calmly unplugging the straighteners and picking me up. I was exhausted and as broken as the pieces of chalky plaster that covered me.

It was time to seek professional help.

I couldn't bear the feelings of loss and the disregard I felt towards my own existence. It was tearing me apart. My head was like a washing machine, overstuffed with clothes and struggling to move forward into rinse mode. I battled daily with decisions and then realised I seemed to be having a two-way conversation with myself. That frightened me .Things were not good. I was losing it.

25

Resuscitation

It took five sessions for the penny to drop. I must have been ready and willing for the help. And it was revolutionary.

I wasn't the daughter who wasn't 'normal', the mother who was a disgrace, a failure or an embarrassment who deserved to be betrayed, not a woman who made bad choices and was incapable of making sound ones for herself or anyone around her. I was none of it. My life of confusion and self-doubt finally made sense.

I had simply been a girl who searched for the love she felt she had been rationed at an early stage, way beyond memory, and had adapted to survive. That adaptation had become my normal and the constant search for love equally so. It explained my urgent and erratic plunge in and out of relationships, like a seal diving frantically for the fish thrown in the pool, in the hope of catching it and making the hand that fed proud.

I had always wanted to make my parents proud. Anyone proud. I wanted to feel like I fit in at least somewhere. I thought back to my early disastrous relationships and viewed them now instead as valuable lessons.

40. I had loved the person I willed him to be, not what he was.

My failed marriages, grabbed at a time when I needed support, when they had shown kindness. I just simply hadn't tested that kindness or love for long enough, hence the inevitable failures.

I didn't know any of this then. I thought this was my normal 'abnormal daughter' behaviour. Now I could see it all clearly, the pieces finally fit.

Each experience had developed me in some way and brought me closer to *my* truth. The events of my life were not embarrassing mistakes, it was not simply me that was 'fucked up' or 'needy.' Other people had responsibility to take, but where I had faced issues head on, many had chosen to run away from them. I had unwittingly learned so much yet had to endure so much pain to eventually unlock that chalice of self-knowledge.

But I had come out stronger. I had made changes in my life while many still trod the old roads and that made me braver, stronger and provided valuable growth in my life.

I understood why I had felt as I did and realised my life was my own, to make my decisions with confidence and to follow my heart and head without the worry of upsetting anyone or being judged. It was okay to act for the interests of me, it was not a sin. And beauty, well that comes from within. If you don't make peace with your own soul it shows externally, but when they work in harmony, the result is magnificent.

I realised I had unwittingly made the most important person proud.

Me.

Handcuffs gone, I could break the shackles and be free.

Without a second to waste, I utilised my blessings.

I launched my own successful property business; life was now too short to work for the success of others or with people not of my choice.

I finally agreed to marry Rod. My soulmate. After seven years of dating and him passing every impossible test I set him, I shattered the habit of impulsive erratic decisions because of course, I now understood and could make good decisions from my heart. I simply and truly adored him. Genuinely. It was not a crime to trust and follow that feeling on the road to happiness.

I stood there at our wedding with my Frankie by my side. My daughters did not respond to their invitation. My family pews were empty aside from three important people. My cousins. Tash, Emma and Ryan. All three travelled miles and sat with smiles that outdid Gnasher from the Beano. Those smiles wrapped around my heart that day and kept me warm. I was no longer alone. For the first time in my life, surrounded by those that loved us, I looked at Rod and I felt like I belonged.

I ended the constant reaching out to my daughters and parents and the associated cycle of rejection and pain. Their thoughts were exactly that and if they did not want me in their lives or love me enough to welcome my happiness and choices, then that was a problem for them, not me. I loved myself enough now to not be dependent on the scraps thrown by others.

While that family door will always remain ajar for if and when they are ready to deal with reality, I refuse to compromise or feel guilty for protecting my own happiness and genuinely smiling again.

I had been reborn.

The local newspaper dropped on the doormat and, as I glanced at it, I stopped dead in my tracks as lady Karma made her third visit.

Slowly, I inhaled deeply before looking skyward,

opening my eyes and whispering, 'Thank you'.

Married police boss, Deputy Chief Constable Carl Langley , who faced the sack over an alleged affair with a police colleague, was permitted to secretly retire.

He was investigated over his relationship with Dyfed Powys's top lawyer , Samantha Gainard and left on the day he completed his 30 years of service, with a full pension. He already caused anger for claiming around £40,000 public money in removal expenses and instead of being suspended and investigated, was moved to a national role on a £125,00 income.

The affair ended but a complaint was made that it may have influenced job applications and promotions.

West Mercia Police investigated and came to the decision he should face misconduct proceedings. The outgoing Chief, Simon Prince, deemed Mr Langley's behaviour was equivalent to Gross Misconduct. A week later Dyfed Powys agreed he could retire and leave without being subject to a disciplinary hearing and thus avoid any public scandal.

Ms Gainard remained suspended until her resignation a few months later.

I recalled my verdict, that Peter and I had *repeatedly accused officers within Dyfed Powys Police of lying and lacking integrity.*

We were not wrong.

Fourteen long years it has taken for me to finally feel able to write my story. In the meantime, I was judged, castigated and branded as something I never was. That *Send* button on the dating site was a destruct button wired to my whole world. I pressed it and it catalysed the obliteration of everything I had.

My career. My blood family. My two children. My life.

Let down by my own flesh and blood and an organisation I trusted.

Outsiders had plenty to say. Plenty of hindsight, but nobody walked in my shoes. Nobody ever will.

Only years later did I gain one important victory out of it all.

The battle of discovery with myself.

On Lady Karma's final visit to date, out of courtesy, I told Dean of my newfound passion for writing. His response was supportive; 'I hope you haven't put anything in there that can identify me. It could affect my work and if that happened, I would not be happy.'

I suppose you wouldn't, would you Dean....No. I think I can identify with that.

But those days of the old Jill are long gone, where my achievements craved the approval of others. There is a new one who now knows herself better than anyone or anything.

And she is strong.

2020 would have been my thirtieth year of service to an organisation that betrayed me when I was at my lowest ebb. I never lied. My only crime was seeking love and to be deceived by a man I thought I knew.

Except he was bank robber and I was Sergeant Jill Evans, number 827 of the Dyfed Powys Police.

Printed in Great Britain
by Amazon